Marriage From Heaven

Secrets to a strong, healthy and passionate marriage

Drs. Uyi & Faith Abraham

Zofaa Publishing
Atlanta, Georgia

© 2018 Uyi & Faith Abraham

Visit

www.MarriageFromHeaven.tv

ISBN-13: 978-1981997824

ISBN-10: 1981997822

All rights reserved.
Printed in the United States of America.

Published by
www.zofaapublishing.com

No part of this publication may be reproduced, sold, emailed, or transmitted in any form without the prior permission of the author except in the case of brief quotations within critical articles and reviews.

Except otherwise quoted, scripture quotations are from the King James Version® © 1982 by Thomas Nelson, Inc. Used by permission. All rights reserved.
Amplified Bible (AMP) Copyright © 1954, 1958, 1962, 1964, 1965, 1987 by The Lockman Foundation. The ESV® Bible (The Holy Bible, English Standard Version®) is adapted from the Revised Standard Version of the Bible, copyright Division of Christian Education of the National Council of the Churches of Christ in the U.S.A. All rights reserved. Scripture quotations marked (MSG) are from *The Message* by Eugene H. Peterson. © 1993, 1994, 1995, 1996, 2000. NavPress Publishing Group. Scripture quotations marked (NLT) are from *Holy Bible*, New Living Translation. © 1996, 2004, 2007. Tyndale House Publishers, Inc. All rights reserved. Scripture quotations marked (CEV) are from Contemporary English Version ® Copyright © 1995 American Bible Society. All rights reserved.
(GW) GOD'S WORD® is a copyrighted work of God's Word to the Nations. Copyright 1995 by God's Word to the Nations. All rights reserved.
Holy Bible, New International Version®, NIV® Copyright © 1973, 1978, 1984, 2011 by Biblica, Inc.® Used by permission. All rights reserved worldwide.

Content

Preface		5

SECRET ONE: God — 15
- Day 1 — It All Starts With God — 16
- Day 2 — Pursue Together — 21
- Day 3 — Prioritizing Your Marriage — 24
- Day 4 — Made To Last Forever — 27

SECRET TWO: Love And Honor — 31
- Day 5 — Understanding Her Needs — 32
- Day 6 — Understand His Needs — 36
- Day 7 — Finding Your Spouse's Love Language — 40
- Day 8 — Out-kind Each Other — 45

SECRET THREE: Baggage — 49
- Day 9 — Identifying Your Baggage — 50
- Day 10 — Letting Go — 56
- Day 11 — Healing From Past Hurts — 59
- Day 12 — Power Of Forgiveness — 66

SECRET FOUR: Communication — 69
- Day 13 — Defining Expectations — 70
- Day 14 — How To Communicate With Your Spouse — 75
- Day 15 — Listen To Hear — 78
- Day 16 — Speaking With Grace — 81

SECRET FIVE: Selflessness — 87
- Day 17 — Serving Each Other — 88
- Day 18 — Power Of Submission — 94

Day 19	Friendship Forever	98
Day 20	Adding Value To One Another	102

SECRET SIX: Boundaries — 107
Day 21	Boundaries And Accountability	108
Day 22	Dos And Don'ts	114
Day 23	The Trust Factor	119
Day 24	Protecting Your Marriage From Intruders	123

SECRET SEVEN: Money — 127
Day 25	Creating Financial Intimacy	128
Day 26	Financial Health	133
Day 27	Budgeting	137
Day 28	The Power Of Generosity	142

SECRET EIGHT: Visioneering — 146
Day 29	Vision Casting For Your Marriage	147
Day 30	Two Becoming One	154
Day 31	Dealing With Compatibility Issues	157
Day 32	The Big Picture	162

SECRET NINE: Family Dynamics — 165
Day 33	Spiritual Forces At Work	166
Day 34	Raising Godly Children	172
Day 35	Dealing With In-laws	176
Day 36	Tips For Blended Families	182

SECRET TEN: Sex — 187
Day 37	Developing Sexual Intimacy	188
Day 38	Spice It Up	193
Day 39	Rekindle The Flame	197
Day 40	Passionate Living	203

Preface

WELCOME to marriage from heaven. Our heart desire is that you will have the foundation of exactly what you need to create a *strong, healthy and passionate* marriage.

This is more than a book; it is a guide to a 40-day marital expedition that will enable you to experience a marriage from heaven.

There are two types of marriages—a *Marriage from Heaven* or a Marriage from Hell. Unfortunately, most married couples are living in a marriage from hell.

A recent statistics showed that 65% of couples said they were *unhappy* with their spouse and *hated* their marriage. That is an alarming number. There is also a crisis of divorce in our generation like never before.

Here is another figure that should trouble you: *50%* of *new marriages* will end in divorce within the first five years.

There is a cry for help in our society and culture regarding marriages. This is why we wrote this book to help you experience a marriage from heaven just like God created it.

MARRIAGE IS SPIRITUAL! God invented the greatest idea EVER, defying mathematics — Two Becoming one!

We know firsthand what it is to have a bad marriage. The first few years of our own marriage were unhealthy, tumultuous, and we almost ended in a breakup, not once but at least three times.

Today, thirteen years in with the help of God and by applying the principles that we now teach in this book and all over the world, we were able to save our marriage. Our marriage is now strong, healthy and passionate. We are on a crusade to save marriages and relationships!

Drawing from research, personal wealth of information, and experiences gained from our private Christian marriage/relationship counseling practice, we wrote this book to help couples WIN by giving them the secrets to a strong, healthy and passionate marriage.

Marriage gets better when you do it right—God's way. A marriage from heaven is a marriage that is built on the principles we are teaching in this book. We strongly believe that the greatest marriage is two servants in love.

Outside of God, the view and perspective on marriage is beneath its potential. It will not reach the point of satisfaction, change, transformation that it has the ability to produce.

We know that every couple is different. And we also understand that what God wants to do within your life, within the context of marriage, will be different from another couple's.

So we do not subscribe to one size fits all, cookie cutter marriage formula. And, honestly, anyone who has a one size fits all mentality toward marriage does not understand the uniqueness of marriage.

But God does have a **foundation** that we can follow and allow to lead and guide us into the type of union He desired for us before the foundations of the world.

Your Next 40 Days

This was written in a way that is completely different from many books out there on the subject of marriage. We've divided this book into 10 secrets or sections, and within each, there are four short chapters (or days) that relate to the secret. These are topics that you can never run away from.

They will always arise during the time that you are sharing your life with your spouse. In some seasons, there are topics that weigh much more heavily than other topics. That is normal. When a particular topic comes to the forefront, you will find that the foundation that has been laid within this book will carry you and give you a healthy and godly vantage point to begin to work from.

Even the best marriages need work. And the worst marriages can become better. There's absolutely nothing that is too hard for two people who decide to be in one accord and work on their marriage.

Your Next 40 Days: The number 40 has a lot of spiritual meaning and significance in the Bible; that is why we decided to make this book into a 40-days reading plan. Whenever God wanted to prepare someone for His divine will, He took 40 days:

- Noah's life was changed by 40 days of rain.
- Moses was transformed by 40 days on Mount Sinai.
- The spies were altered by 40 days in the Promised Land.
- Jesus was empowered by 40 days in the wilderness.

Now it's your turn to be transformed and transfigured.

How To Read This Book

We wrote this book with the intent that you will read it over the next 40 days with your spouse or significant other. Each day, there is a topic related to the main secret you are studying. Each day starts with a Bible verse that teaches a truth from that chapter.

Discussion Questions. At the end of each chapter, there are discussion questions for you both to read and answer together. These questions will help you think about the implications of what you have read and how it applies to you personally and your marriage. We encourage you to write your answers in the margin of the book or in a dedicated notebook.

Group Study

You could also use this book for group study at your church, small group, marriage club, or between your friends.

We strongly urge you to get one or more friends to join you in reading this book during the next 40 days. A journey is always better when it is shared.

With a partner or a small reading group, you can discuss what you read and bounce ideas off each other. This will help you grow stronger and deeper spiritually and in your marriage.

Because we know the benefits, we want to challenge you to stick with this journey to a marriage from heaven for the next 40 days, not missing a single daily reading. Your marriage is worth the investment.

Get this book for a friend, whether they are presently single or married, they will benefit immensely from this book. Friends don't allow friend's marriage to suffer. The divorce rate and numbers of unhappy couples are alarming and troubling. Friends help friends. A gift of *Marriage From Heaven* is one that your family and friends will cherish for a lifetime.

40 Days Marriage Boot Camp

To further strengthen our resolve and commitment to your marriage success, we have made it easier for you to follow along by creating a 40 Days Marriage Boot Camp where you will receive daily beautifully written email newsletters, short videos and marriage coaching. So, in the next forty days, we will be your marriage coaches and pouring into your lives.

A separate registration is required for that.
Go and register and join the program.

www.marriagefromheaven.tv

What about if you had the nation's leading marriage and relationship coaches to be your personal marriage mentors for 40 days? What is the value of that? PRICELESS.

Ultimate Marriage & Relationship Coaching for 40 Consecutive days:
- Daily video coaching
- Personalized email
- Bible verse for the day
- Discussion questions & Much More to help you have HEAVEN in your marriage.

Make it a daily appointment on your schedule. Your marriage is worth it. Your future together is worth it.

Let's sign a covenant agreement together indicating that you will pursue a marriage from heaven that is Strong, Healthy and Passionate.

There is something significant about signing your name to a commitment. If you get a partner to read through this with you, have them sign it too.

Let's get started together!

Love,
Drs. Uyi & Faith Abraham

MY MARRIAGE COVENANT

40 Days of Marriage from Heaven

I commit the next 40 days of my life to improve myself and my marriage.

_____
Your Name & Signature

_____
Your Partner's Name & Signature

_____
Start Date

Uyi Abraham   *Dr. Faith*
_____
Drs. Uyi & Faith Abraham

SECRET ONE

God

Day 1

It all starts with God

Scripture Meditation: "Then the Lord God said, 'It is not good for the man to be alone. I will make a helper who is right for him'" (*Genesis 2:18, GW*).

"If not for God, we would not be married today." That was my shocking admission to my wife one day after a heated argument.

"Well, you sure are right," she responded.

When I married Faith, I'll admit I was looking for a good woman who would serve me, meet my needs and cherish me a kingdom in my own little kingdom. That's what I thought a successful marriage was: finding someone to serve you. That's because that was all I saw growing up in a different country where I was born. I thought men were superior to women.

The first two years of our marriage was not very good, to say the least. You see, we married young, naïve and inexperienced about biblical marriage. We had no marital model to follow. Both of our parents didn't have a strong, healthy and passionate marriages.

In our brokenness and despair, I started considering a way out of the marriage. I was ready for a breakup.

"This felt like a marriage from hell.

"My needs weren't met," I complained to God.

"I don't know how to meet my wife's need," I continued in my prayer.

We had nothing else to help us, so we decided to study the Bible, especially in the scriptures regarding marriage, bought books, attended conferences and took some online marriage courses.

Gradually, the Lord began to do a great work in our hearts. We began to learn what a marriage from heaven looks like and were determined to make it happen for us.

I dropped my faulty thinking and orientation regarding marriage. I understood that marriage wasn't about satisfying my needs only—the greatest marriage is two servants in love. Just like Jesus said that two shall become one—that's the goal of heaven in putting two people together to do life together.

A marriage from heaven starts with God. Putting God first in your marriage is the wisest investment you can ever make in your marriage.

A godless marriage is a marriage from hell.

Whether you are a spiritual person or not, God is the foundation of every marriage. He is the foundation because He created it. Because He created marriage, He alone can teach you how to have a marriage from heaven.

Every successful, satisfying relationship starts with a satisfying relationship with Jesus. As you develop that growing relationship with Jesus, He will fill up your love tank until it overflows. It will be easier for you to love and be loved.

Seeking the face of God will cause a great spiritual growth in you that will have a positive effect on your marriage.

The scripture says, "For I know the plans I have for you, says the Lord. They are plans for good and not for evil, to give you a future and a hope" (*Jeremiah 29:11, TLB*).

Like we said earlier, a growing relationship with Jesus is a must if you're seeking a blessed relationship and marriage. *During tough times, you'll need something stronger than yourself to rely on to remain committed.*

Loving God and having a strong and growing relationship with Jesus is not a requirement for you only but also for your mate. If a person cannot love God, how will they love you?

For God is love.

A good disciple of Jesus makes a good spouse. According to God, marriage is based on covenant. Covenant is not the type of relationship that you go back-and-forth from but rather the type that lasts for a lifetime.

By acknowledging God within your relationship, you acknowledge His standards, His ways and His ideals in the treatment of each other. God's words provide a compass that both parties have to abide by and don't have the power to change.

A strong marriage has God in the midst of it. Experiencing the love of God teaches you what godly love looks and feels like. Also, a fulfilling relationship with Christ takes pressure away from your mate. You won't look for him or her to make you whole because you'll feel complete in Christ.

God desires that every couple live under His blessing and have successful and pleasurable lives. This happens to the extent that couples give and receive grace and truth in their relationship.

When you have God in your relationship, you and your spouse become a three-strand cord that cannot be easily broken. That is because you have now entered into a covenant with God and your spouse.

Discussion Questions

How do you view God within your relationship?

Do you think there is room for God with you and your spouse?

What could you do to deepen your relationship with God within your marriage?

Day 2

Pursue Together

Scripture Meditation: "Brothers and sisters, I can't consider myself a winner yet. This is what I do: I don't look back, I lengthen my stride, and I run straight toward the goal to win the prize that God's heavenly call offers in Christ Jesus" (*Philippians 3:13–14 GW*).

A wise man once told us that *a couple that prays together stays together.* So true!

To have a prosperous marriage, you'll need to pursue God together. One cannot be sluggish in their pursuit of God while the other is on fire. It's amazing how easy marriage is when God is at the center of it. This is the foundation to a healthy marriage. It all starts with God, and you must pursue Him together. When you pursue together, you'll begin to understand why God put you two together. Discovering how God wants to use you and your spouse within His kingdom gives you purpose and binds you as a couple. It's like putting your hand in a glove. You fit together perfectly.

So, today, we are going to share with you three principles that will help you to pursue together in your marriage:

a. Grow Together
The practical way of doing this is engaging in Bible plans together, attending God-centered marriage conferences, serving in your local church and discussing teachings from service. It has a feeling or sentiment of being study partners of God. As you learn more about God, His word, and His standards toward you, it gives you a greater perspective as to how you can love better, summit, and serve each other.

b. Pray Together
Since you are two individuals becoming one, the glue that will hold you together is God. Prayer softens your heart and invites God into the marriage. As you seek God together, you are able to be strong together. When you love God first and partake of His love, it gives you more love to pour out to your spouse. Does that mean that you can't have a good relationship without God? It's possible. It is also very possible that you will be missing out on the depth of

joy, love, wholeness, and happiness that comes from marriage because a marriage without God is operating outside of the realm of its capacity. If someone can have a good marriage 'without God,' imagine how great it can be with Him! Prayer enlarges your marriage.

c. Submit Together

A marriage from heaven is when you submit yourself to Christ, and your spouse submitting themselves to Christ as well, in order to bring about God's purpose for your marriage and you. You benefit from having more things in common with your spouse than not.

The wrong idea of submission is that only the woman submits to her husband. But Christ-like marriages say you should submit to one another in the Lord. We will speak more on this topic in the latter part of this book.

Discussion Questions

1. What could you do together to facilitate growth as a couple?

2. How do you both plan to grow together in the Lord?

3. How are you going to make prayer and Bible study time a priority in your relationship?

Day 3

Prioritizing Your Marriage

Scripture Meditation: "Love is patient. Love is kind. Love isn't jealous. It doesn't sing its own praises. It isn't arrogant" (*1 Corinthians 13:4, GW*).

Isabella was ready to walk out of her marriage. She felt neglected in their 9 month old marriage. Her husband's passion for golf and hanging out with his buddies was tearing their marriage apart.

The irony of their story is that Raul spent three years pursuing Isabella to be his wife. He showered her with attention, kindness, and quality time while they were dating. She could imagine that this was going to be the norm for a lifetime.

But just like in most relationships, we tend to relax a little and get comfortable after we get married.

Raul was destroying not only the marriage but his beautiful bride and didn't even know it. He was failing to prioritize his marriage above his passion for golf. Marriage works best when you prioritize it above all else. You can't give it fifty percent. You'll need to give it a hundred percent.

Your spouse has to feel like they are the most important relationship in your life. And it's your duty to make them feel so.

Marriage is the longest journey in a person's life. If one spouse goes one way, and another goes the other way, it creates conflict and disunity. A husband and wife who constantly serve one another have discovered the secret of a great marriage.

We often teach single people to marry someone who makes them laugh and happy. In the same vein, you should make it your priority to make your spouse laugh and happy.

Looking at the example of Jesus, He prioritized His bride (the church) so much that He gave up His life for her. He put aside all His heavenly glory, power, and grandeur to lay low, humbled himself, served, and ultimately gave His life for His bride.

Raul violated his marriage covenant. His hobby was damaging his dream of a marriage from heaven. His marriage wasn't strong, healthy, or passionate. I remember like it was yesterday we had a session with them.

"So, Raul, what's the most important thing in your life after Jesus?"
"Hmmn ..." There was silence. "Well, my wife and marriage," he said.
"If so, then why are you not making your wife feel so?" I inquired. "Why is she feeling cut off from your love?"

He started to explain himself and gave excuses for his anti-love behavior. After a few sessions with them, their marriage was repaired. Raul and Isabella are happy together. Their marriage is strong and healthy. Passion has returned.

Discussion Questions

1. In what ways have you not prioritized your mate in the past?

2. Beginning today, how do you plan to prioritize your marriage?

3. What is trying to take your focus away from your spouse?

Day 4

Made to Last Forever

Scripture Meditation: "Love never comes to an end. There is the gift of speaking what God has revealed, but it will no longer be used. There is the gift of speaking in other languages, but it will stop by itself. There is the gift of knowledge, but it will no longer be used" (*1 Corinthians 13:8, GW*).

One of the biggest passions of our heart is to take the crusade of the message of this book all across America and the world. God's plan for your marriage is for it to last forever. The love you both share was meant to never go out. As you both continue to pursue God, you will notice that your love for each other deepens.

You can't be happily married with a flaky human love. Human love will fail you in your marriage. Certain things will happen where you'll need the God kind of love in your hearts and soul. You'll need the God kind of love—that is sacrificial and selfless. A divine love is one that prefers the other person. One that is not boastful or arrogant. Let us say it again: *God made marriage to last forever.* No matter what stage or situation your marriage is, your marriage can get better. For a marriage to last forever, you will need:

a. Divine Love
Like we told you earlier, the beginning stages of our marriage were a disaster. Our human love for each other was failing and looking for a way to bail out. But divine love kept us and held our feet to the fire until change came.

b. Give more appreciation
Every human needs to hear words such as "I appreciate you," "I love you."
One man told us, "I get no thanks from my wife, even though I work so hard to provide for her needs." Our advice was, "Give much appreciation to your partner, no matter how little it is. Privately and publicly look for opportunities to praise him/her." Today, you can begin showing appreciation to your partner.

c. Daily Affirmation
We learned in our own marriage that daily affirmation is one of the secrets to a healthy marriage. It's hard to fight when you put your energy toward affirming your spouse. Not only do we affirm each other daily, we also taught the kids to affirm each other. You can hear my husband tell the children: "You guys are so blessed to have a wonderful mother."
Tell your wife daily: "I love you."
Tell your husband every day: "I honor and cherish you."
You will be amazed how your change will change for the best when you affirm, complement and build your mate.

d. Kissing and Physical Touch
We are not trained medical doctors, but from our experience of working with hundreds of couples for over thirteen years, we can tell you that a kiss a day drives marital sickness away. Make it your habit to kiss every day. Now, it doesn't have to be a drawn-out tongue kissing. A simple peck on the lips will do. Touch each other daily. Cuddle, snuggle and flirt. When she walks by you to the kitchen, rub her behind. You will see that she will smile at you.

Discussion Questions

1. How can you make your love last forever?
2. Why is daily appreciation for your spouse important?

3. Discuss the importance of divine love.

Secret TWO
Love and Honor

Day 5

Understanding Her Needs

Scripture Meditation: "Husbands, love your wives, even as Christ also loved the church, and gave himself for it" (*Ephesians 5:25 GW*).

One of the biggest mistakes I made in the early days of our marriage was that I gravely misunderstood my wife's primary need. I thought my primary role in the marriage as a man was to be a *provider*, without realizing what my wife wanted more than anything else was for me to be her *lover*.

The need for *love* is what a woman wants the most in her marriage. Love helps to meet her second primary need, which is *security*. When a woman feels loved by her man, it brings a sense of security and comfort to her. Do you want to experience a marriage from heaven? Then start applying the principles we're giving you. Don't try to reinvent the wheel. Follow the plan of God. God designed women differently than He did men.

Husbands, please know that your wife wants to be close to you. She wants you to listen to her. She wants you to honor and cherish her.

A woman wants your love and attention to be exclusively directed to her.

She doesn't want to share your love tank with another woman. That is why the way you love her can help meet her need for security. Her most secure environment is one in which she is married to a sacrificial, sensitive man.

In Ephesians 5 verse 25, God clearly shows us how to have a marriage from heaven; He says to husbands to love their wives.

God designed men and women with particular needs they are unable to meet on their own. He created marriage, in part, to allow husbands and wives to meet those needs for each other.

Men, Jesus is our ultimate example in loving and serving your bride. Jesus gave His life for you, and you are to follow His model in your marriage. In other words, love her more than you love yourself. Sacrifice and be ready to lay your life for her.

What does a loving husband look like?

· He prays for his wife daily.

· He is dedicated to loving his wife.

· He serves her and her needs.

· He prioritizes her above everyone else.

· He puts her needs above his own.

· He studies his wife to understand her better.

· He affirms her daily with pleasantries and compliments.

· He communicates with her.

· He takes her to church.

· He listens to her and hears her heart.

· He regularly makes sacrifices for her happiness.

Once again, we want to share with you the importance of love and security to a woman. A woman doesn't want to share her man with another woman.

She has to feel secure in her relationship so she can blossom in it. There's no amount of money a man can spend on a woman that can replace the sense of security and exclusivity she needs in that relationship. Make her feel secure in you, and she'll lower her guard and receive you into her heart!

We are on day five of *Marriage From Heaven*. We hope that you're learning the secrets to a strong, healthy and passionate marriage.

Discussion Questions

1. In what ways can you make her feel your love?

2. Describe how Jesus models love in marriage?

3. How would you begin to show sacrificial love to your spouse?

Day 6

Understand His Needs

Scripture Meditation: "Wives, submit yourselves unto your own husbands, as unto the Lord. For the husband is the head of the wife, even as Christ is the head of the church: and he is the savior of the body" (*Ephesians 5:22–23*).

Sarah couldn't understand why her husband of two years was rejecting her advances for intimacy. She cooks; she cleans and contributes financially to the family home. She loves her husband. Yet, her husband was still distant.

She started to believe another woman was involved in the marriage and taking her husband's attention away from her. I will be back to Sarah's story shortly. I need to digress for a minute.

For a man, love is not enough! He has to feel honor and appreciation in his relationship. So, what a man needs above all else from his partner is *honor and appreciation.*

Men and women are completely equal in a marriage, but God created us with different sets of needs. He designed marriage to allow a husband and wife to meet each other's needs.

I respect my husband not only because he is an incredible husband but also because the Bible tells me so. The number one need for men is honor and appreciation. God never designed for men to meet their need themselves.

In Ephesians 5:33, Paul writes, "let each one of you in particular so love his own wife as himself, and let the wife see that she respects her husband." In addition to his command toward men, Paul says a wife should respect her husband.

One thing I know for sure is that men are attracted to honor and appreciation. If he can only get it from work, he'll pour himself into his job and not want to come home. God forbid another woman honors and appreciates your husband more than you do.

Sarah's problem was that she loved her husband, but he didn't feel honored and appreciated by her. So he shut down emotionally and sexually. A man spells LOVE as H-O-N-O-R.

When a man feels disrespected, it is especially hard to love his woman. When a woman feels unloved, it is equally hard to honor her husband.

When a man is disrespected by his woman, he acts out. What men want in a relationship is respect, affirmation, support, and encouragement to continue giving. He needs to feel he is making a difference.

When a man feels under-appreciated, he stops giving support. When a woman appreciates what he does for her, he gets much of the love and encouragement he needs for his own sense of well-being and accomplishment.

The male need for respect and affirmation — especially from his woman — is so hardwired into his nature that most men would rather feel unloved or broke than disrespected or inadequate.

In her widely acclaimed book, *For Women Only*, Shaunti Feldhahn shared a survey that was done on men, and it concluded that *three out of four men* would choose to be *Alone and Unloved* than to be *Inadequate and Disrespected*.

If a man feels disrespected, he is going to feel unloved. To a woman, that means: **If you want your man to feel your love, then you need to ensure that he feels your respect most of all.** I've counseled countless women that didn't respect the men in their lives and wondered why they could never win his heart and love.

A man has to lead in serving his woman's love and security needs, and that will provoke a simultaneous service respect and affirmation from his woman. In other words, if you give a woman enough love and security, she will give more than enough respect and affirmation.

Affirm him daily. Support his dreams and aspirations. Pray for your husband he needs it.

Discussion Questions

1. How would you show and communicate honor to your husband?

2. How would you show and communicate love to your wife?

Day 7

Finding Your Spouse's Love Language

Scripture Meditation: "Be kind to each other, sympathetic, forgiving each other as God has forgiven you through Christ" (*Ephesians 4:32, GW*).

I remember a few years ago I surprised my wife with a very nice brand new Sports Utility Vehicle for her birthday. She was ecstatic and grateful for it. Then a few weeks after that, I was chatting with her and asked her to name some of the things I have done for her that she really appreciated and made her feel special.

I was clueless as to what she would say. Her response shocked me. She started by thanking me for being a great husband and for being sensitive to her needs. Then she started naming when I would wash the dishes, help her with the kids, bring her a bouquet of flower, take the trash out, come home on time to share dinner with her and the kids ... on and on, she went. I was waiting for her to name the SUV she just got, but she never did.

It's not that she didn't appreciate the SUV gift. *Receiving gifts* is important to her, but what is more important to her is the *act of service*. She feels loved when I perform acts of service for her or the children.

My wife's primary love language is acts of service.

> *She appreciates when I <u>do things</u> for her and not just give things to her.*

Dr. Gary Chapman's *The Five Love Languages* is a classic book on love and relationships. According to Dr. Chapman, there are five universal ways that all people express and interpret love.

Through his more than 30 years of couples counseling, Dr. Chapman has noticed specific patterns in the way partners communicate—and it turns out that most of the population express and interpret love in the same five ways, according to his observations.

Here are the 5 love languages:

1. Words of affirmation
For those who prefer the words of affirmation love language, hearing "I love you," "You're an incredible spouse," and other compliments are what they value the most.

They love praises and to be reminded of their place in your life. Affirming words from the one they love hold real value for them. Furthermore, negative or insulting comments can really break down their spirit.

2. Quality time
This language is all about giving the other person your undivided attention. They love when you prioritize spending time with them. Unlike the words of affirmation language, to them, talk is cheap, and being a loved one's main focus leaves quality timers feeling satisfied and comforted.

3. Receiving gifts
Dr. Chapman says for some people, what makes them feel most loved is to receive a tangible gift. This doesn't necessarily mean the person is materialistic, but a meaningful or thoughtful present it was makes them feel appreciated.

4. Acts of service
For these people, actions speak louder than words. People who speak the language of service want their partner to recognize that their life is rough and help them out in any way possible. Lending a helping hand shows you really care. Basically, if you're not willing to show your appreciation by doing them a favor, you're saying you don't value them.

5. Physical touch
To this person, nothing speaks more deeply than appropriate touch. That doesn't mean only in the bedroom—everyday physical connections, like hand holding, kissing, or any type of re-affirming physical contact is greatly appreciated.

A person who speaks the language of physical touch isn't necessarily an over-the-top PDAer, but getting a little touchy-feely does make them feel safe and loved.

The way to your spouse's heart is to find out their primary love language. Guys, learn the secret to your woman's heart. It's the little things you do for her every day that counts more than the one-time big thing you do for her. To keep your woman happy, you'll need to show her love and affection every day and not be a one-hit wonder.

Wow! That's so good. That statement alone is worth every penny you spent on this book. And we mean it!

Discussion Questions

1. What is your spouse's primary love language?

2. What is your primary love language?

3. How can you serve your spouse's primary love language?

Day 8

Out-kind Each Other

Scripture Meditation: "Love is patient. Love is kind. Love isn't jealous. It doesn't sing its own praises. It isn't arrogant" (*1 Corinthians 13:4*).

Marriage gets better when you do it right—God's way. A marriage from heaven is a marriage that is built on the principles of God.

It just baffles us to see two people fall in love and then get married and start hating each other. When you're dating, you fall in love because you make your spouse your top priority. You are so kind to them that they fantasize spending the rest of their lives with you.

You must continue to show that kindness and passion to your spouse like you did before you married if you truly want to have a marriage from heaven.

Passion is not an emotion that should come and go. Treasure your spouse and fall in love again.
Your assignment from today is to love and out-kind each other every day, especially when your spouse seems undeserving of your kindness.

The first two years of our marriage was horrible. We were both selfish and totally unprepared. Our marriage was heading to a breakup. We were arguing a lot and finding it hard to be on the same page on a lot of things. In our study of scripture, we learned one of the secrets to a strong, healthy and passionate marriage — out-kind each other. Wow! It was such a big revolution for us.

We decided we will no longer fight over petty things. We will begin to love and out-kind each other — overwhelm each other with kindness.

What is kindness?

The dictionary defines it as the quality of being friendly, generous, and considerate.

Consideration is one of the best parts of kindness.

Are you considerate of your spouse's feelings before you speak?

Are you considerate of their needs and wants?

Before you do anything, do you take into account how your husband or wife will react?

When you start taking consideration and kindness into thought, you will find out that you are doing a better job as a husband or wife.

Jesus preached about doing unto others as you would want them to do unto you.

Kindness kills every kind of hurt, grudge or misunderstanding in a relationshop. Also your kindness to your mate makes them feel like you love and value them.

A marriage from heaven is a passionate marriage — one where both of you constantly pursue each other with love and kindness. Treasure your spouse. Make them feel like they are worth a billion bucks to you.

Everyone wants to be in love for a lifetime. For many, the dream of lifelong love has become filled with disappointment and heartache. This is because they don't out-kind each other.

Discussion Question

1. Have you been out-kinding your spouse lately?

2. In what ways do you need to improve in pursuing your spouse?

3. How do you plan to be considerate of your spouse's needs and wants?

SECRET THREE

Baggage

Day 9

Identifying Your Baggage

Scripture Meditation: "And it shall come to pass in that day, that his burden shall be taken away from off thy shoulder, and his yoke from off thy neck, and the yoke shall be destroyed because of the anointing" (*Isaiah 10:27 KJV*).

Janet was only seventeen years old when she started dating Tyson. Their relationship was on and off for a few years. They later reconnected in college and married five years later. They picked up great jobs in their city, and everything seemed like it was going fine.

Tyson began to notice that Janet was unhappy most of the time. He couldn't figure out the source of her sadness.

What Tyson didn't realize is that Janet brought some baggage with her to the marriage. She was stuck in a soul tie relationship with her ex.

Now, please listen to us, everyone comes into a marriage with a piece of baggage or two or three. It doesn't matter how holy of a Christian you are; if you look carefully, you can identify a piece of baggage you need to get rid of.

One of the reasons new relationships fail is because we're still stuck in the old ones and don't even know it. Soul ties are invisible bounds that wreak havoc in so many relationships and marriages.

In our counseling office, we regularly identify soul ties as a reason many marriages suffer and some fail.

Remember, the goal of God is for you to have a strong, healthy and passionate marriage.

A healthy marriage is one that is free from baggage.

Marital statistics say that money, poor communication, and sex are the three biggest reasons why marriages end up in divorce. We would like to present another theory, and that theory is unsolved personal issues.

Personal issues cause more divorces than money, poor communication, and sex could ever do combined! Although we don't have the scientific proof to back this up, we have sat down with enough couples to identify the root of a problem. The root will always determine the fruit.

Your baggage might not be that of a soul tie; it might be other personal issues or even generational issues that you brought with you into the marriage.

Let's take the *money issue* for example. If someone had a bad spending habit while they were single, what do you think would happen to that habit when they married?

They bring that same money issue into the marriage. This is one of the reasons why we are very strong proponents of premarital counseling. That exposes the baggage and weakness in you so they can get fixed or healed prior to saying "I do" at the altar.

Initially, one spouse would say that the other is so bad with finances it's jeopardizing their well-being, but upon further inspection, there's a root problem that the spouse is refusing to deal with. That refusal to deal with the root issue causes the fruit of bad

money habits to manifest. The unresolved root issue is the baggage that needs to be unpacked and sorted through in order for the money issue to be resolved.
Marriage is a magnifier. Whatever you don't like about yourself or have an issue working through will eventually come to light. You now have someone who is with you 24 hours a day who can see your faults and weaknesses as clear as day. After a while, they will begin to express their grievances with it. The question is, will you be mature enough to work on them or, if possible, resolve them? Personal improvement requires the precious gifts of patience and forgiveness.

How to know you have a soul tie

Have you found yourself tormented by thoughts about a person, excessively wondering about them, checking on them, rehearsing times with them? If so, you have soul ties. Have you grieved over a severed relationship with someone you were once close to? If so, you have soul ties.

Soul ties are formed through close friendships, through vows, commitments and promises, and through physical intimacy.

Not all soul ties are bad. God wants us to have healthy relationships that build us up, provide wisdom, and give godly counsel. God will

strategically bring good relationships into our lives to form healthy soul ties just like in the case of David and Jonathan. See 1 Samuel 18:1 (AMP).
In contrast, Satan always brings counterfeits into our lives to form unhealthy soul ties.

A few ways unhealthy soul ties can be formed include:
· *Abusive relationships (physically, sexually, emotionally, verbally)*
· *Adulterous affairs*
· *Sex before marriage*
· *Obsessive entanglements with a person (giving them more authority in your life than you give to God)*
· *Controlling relationships*

The dysfunctionality of your upbringing when left unresolved will invariably run your life into the ground. Until you deal with an issue head-on, that issue will continue to deal with you. When you realize that you have unhealthy habits, traits, behaviors, then you must get to the root of those things in order for them to truly leave your life.

So, based on what you know and understand, you have to take certain steps that will allow you to deprogram yourself and then reestablish yourself as who you are supposed to be with functional and healthy habits.

Now your baggage might not be a soul tie. It may be fear, anxiety, depression, lust, procrastination, addiction, laziness, self-abuse, domineering, controlling or whatever. Find your baggage. Identify your baggage before it bleeds into your relationship and causes a wreck.

Self-denial is the worst form of denial. It blinds you to your issues so they never get fixed. Please don't be so self-righteous that you don't see your baggage.

We want you to identify whatever baggage you carried into the marriage and get help, deliverance, prayer, or counseling to root it out.

You cannot have a healthy relationship until you are healthy!

Discussion Questions

1. What baggage did you bring into the marriage that you haven't yet told your husband/wife?

2. What process have you taken to identify the baggage in your life?

3. How do you plan to help your spouse overcome their baggage?

Day 10

Letting Go

Scripture Meditation: "Therefore we also, since we are surrounded by so great a cloud of witnesses, let us lay aside every weight, and the sin which so easily ensnares us, and let us run with endurance the race that is set before us" (*Hebrews 12:1, NKJV*).

One of the most difficult things to do is to let go of the baggage we carry. We carried them for so long that they've now become a part of us.

We've seen couples claim a piece of baggage and make it their identity.

One Christian man said to us the other day, "I am just an angry man. That's who I am, and I've been this way since birth."

But the problem is that no one was born angry. Anger is not a fruit of the Holy Spirit. Anger is a spirit, and it's of the devil. A Christian should never have the spirit of anger in them. Also know that some spirits such as anger can be inherited and passed on from generation to generation.

Here is what Paul said in Galatians 5:22-23 (AMP): "But the fruit of the Spirit [the result of His presence within us] is love [unselfish concern for others], joy, [inner] peace, patience [not the ability to wait, but how we act while waiting], kindness, goodness, faithfulness, gentleness, self-control. Against such things there is no law."

The Christian man we are talking about lived with anger for over 40 years, and it was hard for him to let go—that's all he knew. The problem is that marrying an angry man is a marriage from hell.

Anger unsolved often leads to rage, verbal abuse, physical abuse, addictions, gambling or even worse.

An unhealthy partner cannot build a strong, healthy and passionate marriage. You have to be willing to change, not only for your sake but also for the sake of your spouse.

Letting go can be one of the most arduous works to do. But the results are well worth it. Often times people don't realize that the events of their past are still raging within their hearts. These events cause a leak. There's also the baggage that will take someone to the altar prematurely seeking fulfillment and happiness in the arms of their spouse beyond what any spouse can provide.

Some of that baggage includes but is not limited to former unhealthy and toxic relationships, the relationship that our parents had with each other (if there was one at all), and dysfunctional personal behaviors and habits. These are all pieces of baggage that can weigh us down and put a strain on your marriage.

Now here is the hard part: Will you let go of the baggage?

Are you willing to forgive? Are you willing to get counseling or therapy, depending on how traumatic the events were? Can you openly admit that there is some inner work that you need to do? People can easily draw the conclusion that marriage doesn't work, but the real problem is the two people not working their inner issues for the marriage to work.

Discussion Questions

1. What are some baggage you need to let go?

2. Do you think you need professional help to let go?

Day 11

Healing From Past Hurts

Scripture Meditation: "He healeth the broken in heart, and bindeth up their wounds" (*Psalms 147:3, KJV*).

Uyi and I entered marriage with deep emotional wounds and selfish expectations. We didn't know that marriage wasn't about an individual getting all their needs met at the expense of the other.

As we look back now, we realize that at the time we married, we were both emotionally unhealthy. We were like two porcupines trying to love each other. The closer we got, the more we hurt each other.

Thirteen years in, thank God we have grown so well together that now we have a strong, healthy and a passionate marriage.

We are truly living a marriage from heaven, and we believe that you can experience that too. That's why we wrote this book to help individuals and couples like you.

We are designed by God to love our spouse passionately, permanently, intimately, totally and unconditionally.

As pastors, we understand that a church cannot grow beyond the emotional health of its pastor, and we believe the same is true for a marriage: your relationship with your spouse will never exceed your individual emotional health.

It is very sad to note that most churches shy away from topics of emotional health.

If you are happy in your marriage, you will be happy. But if you are not happy in your marriage, it does not matter what else is good in your life. You will not be happy, and then you will make everyone around you unhappy.

When divorcing couples go before a judge, it is common to hear them cite *irreconcilable differences* as the reason for their divorce. Yet, the truth is that most divorces are as a result of emotional unhealthiness in one or both partners.

Marriage will test your emotional health and strength like no other.

There will be days when your spouse will push you to the extreme — either by their words, attitude, action or behavior. But because you are emotionally healthy and have dropped those baggage, you can handle the situation much better than others.

Please note that emotional healthiness takes time. It always takes patience and experience in knowing how to read, understand and love your mate.

Today, our marriage is blessed. We are in love with each other. We lead a peaceful, joyful and strong marriage. But it didn't happen overnight. It took months and months of prayer and working on us to get here.

Uyi: "One of the areas of my emotional unhealthiness in the early days of our marriage was that I shut down when I disagreed or was upset with my wife. I would not say a word, would not look at her, and try to distance myself as much as I could for sometimes days in a stretch.

"I took disagreement as personal rejection (a sign of emotional unhealthiness). When things didn't go my way at church or the office, I brought it home and kept a horrible attitude around the house."

Signs of Emotional Unhealthiness

He/she cannot control their emotions.

He/she is led by their emotions rather than by their personal strength.

He/she personalizes disagreements as rejection.

He/she lacks the willpower to say No when they need to say no.

He/she seeks revenge and likes to pay back.

He/she is a people pleaser.

He/she wants to win every argument at the other person's expense.

He/she is bound by past hurts, malice, bitterness, and unforgiveness.

He/she is weak in their morals, conviction, or safety.

He/she fails to take responsibility for their action.

Uyi: "One by one, I began. I started to tackle every root, hurt, and baggage that was wrecking my life and marriage.

"Let me say again, it wasn't easy. It took a while. I had to admit that I was emotionally unhealthy and cried out for help."

How do you get and stay emotionally healthy?

1. Learn to be proactive in your emotions and not reactive.
2. Communicate your feelings.
3. Have the attitude of a servant partner.
4. Continuously purge your soul of self.
5. Always be patient with yourself and with others.
6. Prayer and meditation.
7. Forgive quickly.

God wants to use your scars and pain to heal your life, marriage and help other people. Will you let Him change you today so that your marriage can be healthy? Then it begins by realizing that healing is a partnership and a process, not just a one-time event.

May God give us the grace to develop marriages that are a sign and wonder, marriages that point to Jesus and offer a visible picture of the depth of God's love for the world.

A soul tie is an emotional bond or connection that unites you with someone else in your past or present.

You can become bound to a person through your soul.

Breaking Soul Ties

There are 4 Key steps to breaking soul ties:

1. Acknowledge
2. Confess and Repent
3. Forgive
4. Break and Remove

Pray this prayer aloud to help you break free from unhealthy soul ties: Lord God, I boldly approach Your throne of grace, covered in the shed blood of Your Son. In Jesus' mighty name, I ask You to cut any and all ungodly soul ties between myself and anyone else created by any relationship, sexual or otherwise, known or unknown, remembered or forgotten. I decree, declare and prophesy that I am free from all new and past ungodly soul ties in Jesus' name. Amen!

You can also pray and break the covenant of ungodly soul ties by calling out the name of the person you need to be free from.

Pray like this: Lord God, In Jesus' name, I break and destroy any and all ungodly soul ties between myself and __(the person's name here)_____. I free myself from that covenant, and I completely give my heart, soul, and body to You, Jesus! Amen!

Please note that until you break and untangle old, unhealthy soul ties, you're not ready for a new, healthy relationship. Do not carry past baggage into a new relationship.

Discussion Questions

1. How would you rate your emotional healthiness from 1 to 10 — and 10 being the highest?

2. Can you identify any baggage that you have been dragging around?

2. Have you noticed any root issues in your life that you have been neglecting to deal with?

3. How can your spouse help or support you in dealing with any emotional unhealthiness?

Day 12

Power Of Forgiveness

Scripture Meditation: "If you forgive the failures of others, your heavenly Father will also forgive you. But if you don't forgive others, your Father will not forgive your failures" (*Matthew 6:14–15, GW*).

Lakeisha had felt resentment and anger toward her husband, Tyrone, ever since she found out he had been communicating with his ex-girlfriend Nene through Facebook and text messages. Tyrone had expressed remorse, apologized, and accepted responsibility for his actions, but Lakeisha was unwilling to forgive him.

Over the last six months, Lakeisha had shut down sexually and emotionally. She's been giving Tyrone the silent treatment and unwilling to accept his apologies and desire for counseling and restoration of their marriage. What she didn't realize was that unforgiveness toward her husband was ruining her marriage. We understood the pain of betrayal she was dealing with. Her trust for him was shattered by his actions.

Betrayal by a spouse is the worst form of betrayal.

Marriage is for lovers and forgivers. Forgiveness is a strength and not a weakness. When we let go of wrongs, we loosen Satan's grasp on our relationships.

Forgiveness, contrary to popular belief, does not say that the person who did the wrong was right, but rather it says you will free yourself from the burden of carrying the wrong that was done to you.

A marriage from heaven is not a perfect marriage; rather, it's one for partners who are equal opportunity forgivers. In marriage, one of the invisible reasons that couples begin to loathe each other and lose interest in one another is unforgiveness.

What they said or didn't say. What they did or didn't do. How they responded or didn't respond. Without constant forgiveness, the love of your life will turn into the hate of your life because unforgiveness poisons our perception of our spouse and life. We're not saying overlook the obvious, but we are saying to keep the fire burning and the love alive, healthy doses of forgiveness are necessary.

Sometimes it's not what your spouse says or does that's ruffling your feathers; it's the unforgiveness that's in your heart.

"Recent studies have shown that forgiveness is an essential component of successful romantic relationships. In fact, the capacity to seek and grant forgiveness is one of the most significant factors contributing to marital satisfaction and a lifetime of love," The studies concluded.

Couples who practice forgiveness can rid themselves of the toxic hurt and shame that holds them back from feeling connected to each other.

No matter what he/she did to you, forgive and forget. Do it for you and for your marriage. Forgiveness is about giving yourself, your children, and your partner the kind of future you and they deserve—unhampered by hurt and anger.

Discussion Questions

1. Have you ever dealt with unforgiveness in your heart toward your spouse?

2. In what areas do you need forgiveness from your mate?

3. Why is forgiveness so important?

SECRET FOUR
Communication

Day 13
Defining Expectations

Bible Summary: "But let your communication be, Yea, yea; Nay, nay: for whatsoever is more than these cometh of evil" (*Matthew 5:37, KJV*).

Bruce and Carol have been married for five years. In the last four years, they've been sleeping in different rooms in their condo. Bruce vacated his marital bedroom just barely a year into their marriage and has been sleeping on the couch in the living room ever since.

They barely interacted with each other except to discuss by text messages certain essentials relating to finance or the upkeep of their beautiful three-year-old twin daughters.

Carol was done with the marriage and ready to file for divorce when one of her friends who read my book *No Time To Settle: The Five Rules Of Love, Sex & Dating* recommended that they speak with me — since I am a relationship coach, I might be able to save their marriage.

Their first session with me was very exhausting — jam-packed with accusations and counter-accusations, pointing of fingers, and just talking over each other. The husband and wife each trying to convince me the other person was the problem in their marriage. They were so self-righteous in their ways that they just couldn't hear each other.

After about forty-five minutes into their tirade, I finally interjected.
"OK, I've heard you guys," I summoned. "None of you is the devil in this relationship. In fact, you both love each other; hence the passion in your voice."
Their eyes widened. They couldn't believe what they were hearing.
Here was the problem in their marriage — communication!

Bruce and Carol entered into the marriage without properly communicating their needs, expectations, and desires. They thought time would strengthen it out. Time didn't.

To have a marriage from heaven, you'll have to communicate freely with your husband or wife. They are not a guru or physic. They can't read your mind or thoughts. *Don't expect them to do what you haven't clearly communicated to them.*
Communication is the essential element of every great marriage. Getting to know another human being requires talking. It's how we fall in love. It's how we understand another person's heart. It's how we resolve problems and discuss needs. It's so important.

God gave us mouth and ear so we can communicate with each other.

Good communication is one of the secrets of a strong marriage. Many marriages could be saved if spouses improved the ways they communicate with each other. It's often the simplest bad habits that get couples into trouble. Once a marriage gets on a rough track, negativity grows.

Defining expectations means you talk about everything that matters to you to your spouse. Share how many children you would like to have, where you would like to retire. Do you like to have a dog in the house or a cat? Would you like flowers every week?
Take the time to talk to each other. Tell your spouse what you like and don't like. Let them know the

things about them that trouble you and give them room to improve in those areas.

Underlying each of the issues that you and your spouse disagree about are central questions about care and trust in your relationship.

Good Communication deflects conflicts.

You cannot have a healthy marriage without good communication. Many broken marriages lie in the wake of good people invested in winning the argument who lose sight of their love for each other.

Conflicts arise in the relationship when we don't communicate well. Learn to listen to each other, not only to hear but to understand that they are trying to say to you. Learn how your spouse likes to hear and communicate that way to them.

One day, my wife taught me a very powerful lesson on how to communicate to her.

In the past, I would speak like this, "Babe, you forgot to do the dishes. The floor is unswept, and I can't find my pair of orange dress shoes."

What my wife was hearing was a lack of appreciation on the things she did right and a focus on the things she did wrong. She felt I was chastising her. So I learned to use the rule of *Commend and Correct*. That means I will commend first before I correct. So, if I am trying to bring her attention to something she didn't do right, I start first by thanking and appreciating her for being an excellent wife and always being a blessing to my life, and then I can correct. This simple switch of communication techniques has greatly helped our marriage and made it strong.

Just a sidebar: never talk down to your spouse.

So, the next time conflict knocks on your door, remember that how you communicate is very important.

Discussion Questions

1. In what areas of your marriage do you need to improve on communication?

2. Why is it never good to speak down to your spouse?

3. In what areas of your relationship do you need to define your expectations?

4. Are you free to communicate your heart with your spouse?

Day 14

How To Communicate To Your Spouse

Scripture Meditation: "Let your speech be always with grace, seasoned with salt, that ye may know how ye ought to answer every man" (*Colossians 4:6*).

Previously, I shared with you about the story of Bruce and Carol. Their marriage was failing because of bad communication. After a few counseling sessions on communication, they got their marriage back on track.

Bruce moved back into the bedroom, and their bond is now becoming like a marriage from heaven.

One lady asked me, "Why is it that my husband doesn't know how to communicate with me?" "None of us were born from our mother's womb knowing how to communicate," I responded.

Learning how to communicate with your spouse is going to take time and patience. We will provide you with some tools to help speed the training process.

Here are some communication techniques to use:

1. Never yell at your spouse
Yelling is a childish way to express yourself to your spouse. You should practice to never raise your voice at them. *Remember, you are speaking to your spouse and not your child.* When you feel angry, you should withhold your emotions inside so you don't lash out at your husband or wife.

2. Don't raise your voice
When you can keep your emotions in check, your message can really shine through. This doesn't mean you should try to shove your emotions out of the way. They may be a very important part of your situation. But remember, the whole point of communicating is to be clearly understood. To do that, your channel of communication must go two ways. Excessive emotion interferes with that.

3. Sit down when having tough conversations
What my wife and I found out was that it's very difficult to sit and fight. Boxers and MMA fighters understand this principle very well. That is why they stand to fight. So, in marriage, it's a visioneering

principle for us to never stand when having heated conversations, exchanges or differences of opinion. So, when tensions are arising, we sit and try to reason together or at least understand each other's opinions. Learn to sit and talk.

4. Speak with grace and gentleness
Many people speak too harshly to their spouse. That behavior doesn't glorify Christ. Speak with love and gentleness. Let your words build up and affirm. Your words filled with grace and seasoned with salt. You can improve your relationship today, right now, by putting into practice some of these tips for improving the communication in your relationship:

1. Listen to hear their heart.
2. Listen more than you speak.
3. Speak freely and honestly.
4. Pay attention to nonverbal signals.
5. Be present.

Discussion Questions

1. Which of the communication techniques mentioned is your favorite?

2. Give practical ways you can speak to your spouse with grace.

Day 15

Listen To Hear

Scripture Meditation: "Remember this, my dear brothers and sisters: Everyone should be quick to listen, slow to speak, and should not get angry easily" (*James 1:19, GW*).

The first two years of our marriage was the most difficult ones. My husband and I married young. Fresh and ignorant of what it takes to have a blissful marriage. We didn't know the secrets to having a strong, healthy and passionate marriage. This book, *Marriage from Heaven,* hadn't been written. We had no good book or mentor to teach us how to communicate with each other.

In the last chapter, we dealt with baggage and how it can hold us back in our marriages. I brought a baggage of hurt with me into the marriage, and this prevented me from hearing my husband's heart in certain instances. Sometimes, your baggage can be your filter. That is how you hear and often misinterpret what is being expressed to you.

Listening is an active form of communication and often the most difficult part of it.

In the beginning of your relationship, your marriage is like most—it began with good listening skills. You talked and talked and listened to each other. Years later, it became more and more problematic to listen and hear what is being spoken to you.

Today, my husband and I are not just telling you to listen; we are teaching you to hear the heart of your spouse. It is possible to listen but not hear what the speaker is trying to communicate to you. Listen to hear. Pay full attention. Be focused and be there.

Be patient. Don't interrupt. Let them finish their point before you interject.

It's also important that the words spoken are encouraging and uplifting. Let's be honest here; no more wants to listen to a spouse who nags all the time and talks down to them. Your speech should be filled with kindness, praise, and compliments.

Without positive words spoken, you won't have a very good relationship — or a strong marriage.

One of a woman's most important needs is communication. It's as important to women as sex is for men. Sadly, most men don't realize this until they are taught. Patient and loving communication connects a woman to her world. I had to teach my husband how to communicate to me. Thank God I have a husband who is willing to learn, grow, and become better. When our communication improved, our marriage got stronger.

As you already know, I (Dr. Faith) run a full-service Christian counseling practice, and my specialty is in marriage, family and child therapy. I got a Ph.D. in it.

I often give two instructions to married couples. Women should be more (sexy) sexual than they feel. But on the other hand, I tell men that they should talk more than they feel. Your wife deserves more than a lazy one or two grumbled words at the end of the day.

Discussion Question

1. Why is it important to listen to hear?

2. How do you become better at listening and hearing?

Day 16
Speaking With Grace

Scripture Meditation: "The mouth of the righteous person reflects on wisdom. His tongue speaks what is fair" (*Psalms 27:10, GW*).

Caring is a very important part of communication. It's impossible to communicate with a person who doesn't care. We show how much we care through listening, eye connections, attentive body language, and feedback.

Speaking with grace means to speak in a healthy, loving and kind way to your spouse every time, regardless of how you feel at the present moment.

Healthy couples don't speak from their emotions. They speak from their heart that is full of the love of Christ. They speak to affirm and edify their spouse at all times. Of course, we can't always avoid negative discussions in marriage, but we have to produce those with positive words. Focus on each other's strengths and not weakness.

When you say something that hurts your spouse be quick to say, " I'm sorry."

Focus on the attributes that first made you fall in love. I always tell people they should speak seven positive words for every negative one.

For a healthier communication, try to:

- **Find the Right Time**
  If something is bothering you, and you would like to have a serious conversation about it, make sure you pick the right time to talk. Don't interrupt your partner when they're watching a sports game, TV show, about to go to sleep, or stressed about an upcoming test. Tell your partner you would like to talk later and find a time when you're in the same room and not doing anything important.

- **Talk Face to Face**
  Avoid talking about serious matters or issues in writing. Text messages, letters, and emails can be misinterpreted. Talk in person so there aren't any unnecessary miscommunications.

- **Do Not Attack**
 Even when we mean well, we can sometimes come across as harsh because of our word choice. Using 'you' can sound like you're attacking, which will make your partner defensive and less receptive to your message. Instead, try using 'I' or 'we.' For example, say "I feel like we haven't been as close lately" instead of "You have been distant with me."

- **Be Honest**
 Agree to be honest. Sometimes, the truth hurts, but it's the key to a healthy relationship. Admit that you aren't always perfect and apologize when you make a mistake instead of making excuses. You will feel better, and it will help strengthen your relationship.

- **Check Your Body Language**
 Make eye contact when speaking. Sit up and face your partner. Let your partner know you're listening. Show them you really care. Don't take a phone call, text, or play a video game when you're talking. Listen and respond.

- **Use the 48 Hour Rule**
 If your partner does something that makes you angry, you need to tell them about it. But you don't have to do so right away. If you're still hurt 48 hours later, say something. If not, consider

forgetting about it. But remember, your partner can't read your mind. If you don't speak up when you're upset, there is no way for them to apologize or change. Once you do mention your hurt feelings, and your partner sincerely apologizes, let it go. Don't bring up past issues if they're not relevant.

How to Communicate if You Are Angry

It's okay to get angry in a relationship—everyone does at some point! What's important is that you resolve conflicts in a healthy way. If you get angry with your partner, here are a few steps to take:

- **Stop.** If you get really angry about something, stop, take a step back and breathe. Give yourself time to calm down by watching TV, talking to a friend, playing a video game, taking a walk, listening to some music, or whatever helps you relax. Taking a break can keep the situation from getting worse.

- **Think.** After you're no longer upset, think about the situation and why you got so angry. Was it how your partner spoke, or something they did? Figure out the real problem; then think about how to explain your feelings.

- **Talk.** Finally, talk to your partner, and when you do, follow the tips above.

- **Listen.** After you tell your partner how you feel, remember to stop talking and listen to what they have to say. You both deserve the opportunity to express how you feel in a safe and healthy environment.

It may feel good to unleash your tension on your spouse when they upset you, but the sense of satisfaction is often short-lived. Whatever you say in your angry state is likely to add fuel to the fire.

Yelling at your spouse becomes a quick and easy option, although it often causes more trouble than relief. At some point, emotions need to be communicated in a way that allows you to move past them, not fuel them.

Take your spouse viewpoint and make their day awesome.

Discussion Questions

1. What is the best way to communicate when you are angry?

2. Why is it so important to speak grace to your spouse?

3. Describe some healthy communication tips.

SECRET FIVE
Selflessness

Day 17

Serving Each Other

Scripture Meditation: "Be sincere in your love for others. Hate everything that is evil and hold tight to everything that is good" (*Romans 12:9, CEV*).

When I married Faith, I'll admit I was looking for a good woman who would serve me and fulfill my needs. That's what I thought would make me happy in my marriage. I reasoned, *I'm the king of the castle, so I need to be served.*

I also thought wrongly that my primary role as a husband is to be a provider instead of being a *lover*.

If I can just make enough money and pay her bills and the household bills, then I'm a good husband, I thought to myself.

Needless to say, the idea of me serving my beautiful Faith was the farthest thing from my mind. It was a shock to me that she would even expect me to do anything.

When Jesus washed His disciples' feet, He was setting an example for us to follow. His disciples represented the church—His bride. He washed His bride's feet.

Back in the day, the disciples went all day wearing sandals on dusty roads. Their feet were dirty and filthy. Yet, Jesus didn't care about how dirty or filthy their feet were; He simply stooped low and washed and cleaned their feet.

Jesus preached that the servant was the greatest of all. A husband and wife who constantly serve one another have discovered the secret of a strong, healthy and passionate marriage.

We can't tell enough how revolutionary the concept of serving each other changed our marriage forever. We wake up in the morning thinking of ways to out-serve, out-love and out-kind each other.

Selflessness is one of the greatest secrets to a marriage from heaven.

It is impossible for a couple who practice the concept of selflessness and serving one another to head to the divorce court. The opposite of selflessness is selfishness. Selfishness is the real reason for unhappy, weak, unhealthy and crazy marriages.

Say "No" to Selfishness.

Selfishness makes the marriage all about you — your needs, your wants, your desires, your happiness. It's all you, you, and you.

Selfishness is when you put yourself and interest first before your spouse or the marriage.

Please listen, marriage was never meant to be all about you. It's a holy union instituted by God for two people to enjoy life together and do the will of God.

Pour your time, assets, and abilities into serving your spouse, and your spouse will be drawn to you in a deep and intimate way. Continually investing and adding value to each other helps you stay passionate about each other. It means you're sharing your life with each other. It brings you closer.

God has a purpose for your marriage. Your marriage is helping to accomplish the will and kingdom of God on the earth. God decided it was not good for Adam to be alone, and so He made a compatible helper for him.

He created us for each other. You were made for your spouse and vice versa. I can't achieve what God has premeditated for me without Faith. She can't reach her full potential and glory without me. That is how God decided to do marriage.

The best marriages are made of two servants in love.

Put each other first, and you'll discover the marriage of your dreams.

Your spouse has more to offer you in the marriage when you learn how to serve him/her.

A marriage from heaven is when two people become one heart, mind and body.

Don't hold back.

It surprises us to see many couples who hold back from one another. They hold back love, affection, and finances from each other. Don't do that—*that is a marriage from hell.* If your spouse is selfish, get them help quickly. They need to first read this book, and if they need further help, see a good marriage counselor or coach. Of course, if you are the one who is still bound with self-centeredness, you need deliverance quickly, and get the same help we recommended earlier.

Get rid of these words: 'I,' 'Me,' 'Mine,' and 'Yours.' Those words have crippled many marriages and sent them to the divorce court.

What belongs to you also belongs to your spouse and vice versa. You got it?

Marriage is not meant for selfish people.

In God's design, we can't withhold from each other. This includes sex or any other area. We must give everything we have to each other and share everything completely. The only way two different individuals can become one is if both of us are willing to take what was ours individually and now surrender it to the common cause.

That is the kind of marriage that God blesses. Pastor Jimmy Evans wrote in one of his articles on couples serving each other, "This principle stands in stark contrast to marriage in our modern society. Rather than surrendering and sharing with a sacrificial, servant spirit — couples are more selfish and independent than ever. It is 'my' body 'my' money 'my' — career, etc. The bottom line is this — the word 'my' destroys the spirit of marriage. The word 'ours' creates the spirit of marriage."

Marriage is about sharing our lives with each other.

That requires giving of ourselves and caring for each other. It means we don't make decisions without the agreement of our spouses. It means we don't withdraw anything intentionally to punish or control. It means all of the money and assets of the family belong to both spouses equally, regardless of where they came from or who went to work to earn them.

When you start serving and sharing your lives, you'll be amazed to see how strong, healthy and passionate your marriage will be.

Discussion Questions

1. How do you plan to serve your spouse?

2. Have you been selfish towards your spouse?

Day 18

The Power Of Submission

Scripture Meditation: "Submitting yourselves one to another in the fear of God" (*Ephesians 5:21, KJV*).

Paul (a client of ours) couldn't understand why his newly wedded wife was having a problem with the idea of submission.

It is hard for a woman to submit and surrender her life to a man who's not serving her.

God's idea of submission goes both ways. You should submit to one another.

But now, listen because we are about to tell you something you might have difficulty accepting:

Marriage is for mutual submission, yet the man is the undisputed leader and head of the home. He is not called by God to use this privilege to control, punish, or manipulate his bride. No!

Remember, he is first and foremost a servant leader called and anointed by God to lead his home in holy reverence and love. He has to be more concerned about meeting his wife's need before he thinks of his own.

Here is what the Bible says about this:

"A wife should put her husband first, as she does the Lord. A husband is the head of his wife, as Christ is the head and the Savior of the church, which is his own body. Wives should always put their husbands first, as the church puts Christ first" (*Ephesians 5:22−24, CEV*).

We want to repeat again: **the man is the head of the home in divine partnership with his wife.**
This holy concept for marriages is so spiritual that no human can attain this kind of love and serving without the help and power of God.

Selfishness and independence destroy the spirit of marriage. Giving and sharing create the strongest bond of intimacy possible. We encourage you to consider this point related to your own marriage. It is an area we can all grow in.

See Ephesians 5, verses 25–27 (CEV): "A husband should love his wife as much as Christ loved the church and gave his life for it. He made the church holy by the power of his word, and he made it pure by washing it with water. Christ did this, so that he would have a glorious and holy church, without faults or spots or wrinkles or any other flaws."

Two people becoming one heart, one home, and one mind as they lay aside their individualism and selfishness is what a strong marriage is about.

Who does more of the submission?

The Bible calls the wife to do more of the submission as the best way to prevent conflict and division in the house. So, the wife should yield to her husband's leadership when there is a conflict of idea or direction in the marriage. Simply let him lead.

Here is John Piper's definition of submission: *Submission is the defined calling of a wife to honor and affirm her husband's leadership, and so help to carry it through according to her gifts.*

What submission is Not

1. Submission is not manipulation or control.

2. Submission is not agreeing on everything.

3. Submission does not mean leaving your brain at the altar.

4. Submission is not following blindly.

5. Submission is not condoning abuse.

6. Submission is not losing your own uniqueness, personality, and trait.

If a man's focus in the marriage is all about his wife submitting to him, then the priority of the marriage is lost. For a successful marriage, a husband and wife must find a way to avoid this trap of maintaining superiority. The only way to do this is by sacrifice.

Discussion Questions

1. Is it easy for you to submit to your spouse?

2. In what areas of your marriage do you need to submit more?

3. Do you agree with the concept of mutual submission with the man at the headship of the home?

Day 19

Friendship Forever

Scripture Meditation: "In the same way, a husband should love his wife as much as he loves himself. A husband who loves his wife shows that he loves himself"
(*Ephesians 5:28, CEV*).

Have you and your spouse ever felt like you're growing apart? Even if your interests are very different, you can rediscover the friendship and closeness you experienced at the beginning.

Since we started learning and practicing the principles we are teaching you in this book, our marriage has truly been a marriage from heaven.

We learned that developing *great friendship* is the Secret of Lifelong Passion and Intimacy.

Sadly, many couples experience a thrilling passion that lasts for a while and then slowly fades away.

Every couple can keep the passion alive in their marriage for a lifetime by *daily* building an atmosphere for intimacy to grow — friendship.

Friends don't fight!

Think about that statement again, "Friends don't fight." When you both are best of friends, loving and serving one another, you'll build a passionate relationship and marriage.

Here's another thing: *friends love to help friends succeed.*

Instead of trying so hard to change him/her, learn to make them your friend. Also be their friend.

Great friends make passionate lovers and cute babies.

Selflessness is a trait of friends while selfishness destroys great friendships.

Friends forgive!

Remember: Forgiveness is not optional for the Christian. God *requires* that you forgive your spouse and not hold grudges. If this is a struggle for you, begin by asking the Lord to help you in those areas where you're finding it difficult to forgive.

Friends give up things for friends!

Sometimes, you have to give up certain interests — football, golf, shopping, longer days at work — for the good of your marriage. I have to work less if I am going to make my wife and children happy.

I've always enjoyed working and creating, but my wife and kids want to spend more and more time with me, so I have decided to get off work a little earlier so I can spend more time with the family.

Time is the essential commodity of relationships. For a healthy marriage, we have to take time away from self-focused pursuits and devote it to our spouse.

One of the best ways to deepen the friendship in your relationship is to spend a lot of time together, serving and enjoying each other's company.

The secret of being friends is meeting the need of your spouse that you don't have. Unmet needs open the door for the devil to attack the marriage. Anything other than God that is trying to take your attention away from your spouse is a 'marriage intruder,' and you must stop them.

10 Simple Ways to Strengthen the Friendship in Your Marriage:

1. Make a heartfelt decision to make your spouse your best friend.

2. Take the actions that will bring you both closer.

3. Make date nights a priority.

4. Pray for your spouse daily.

5. Make your friendship unconditional.

6. Take the time to find common interests and then engage in them.

7. Affirm one another daily. Be kind.

8. Be transparent and open with one another.

9. Do what makes him/her happy.

10. Celebrate each other's differences and uniqueness.

Discussion Questions

1. How do you plan to strengthen the friendship in your marriage?

Day 20

Adding Value To One Another

Scripture Meditation: "Just as iron sharpens iron, friends sharpen the minds of each other" (*Proverbs 27:17, CEV*).

"What's the point of being with someone if they can't teach you anything or add any value to your life?"

That was the question one woman asked me after hearing me speak about my book for singles, *No Time To Settle: The 5 Rules Of Love, Sex and Dating*.

I said in the book, "Can they make you better in any way? That should be a foremost question in your mind as you contemplate a dating relationship. Ideally, you should grow together.

When you're deciding whether to stay in a relationship or not, ask yourself this question ... what has my time with this person taught me? Can he/she continue to contribute to my life and my goals?"

One of the tenets of the book teaches that singles should only marry those who can add value to their lives in some way.

This lady was so moved by the teaching that she cornered me to ask me the question. She went on to tell me how her husband doesn't add any value to her life. She claimed she is so lonely and unhappy in her relationship. I could understand her plight. It's an uphill task being married to someone who doesn't make any tangible contribution to your life.

You see, when I married my wife, I made a vow to make her life much better, happier and satisfying that before she met me.

Thirteen years in at the time of this book, and that vow and commitment has never changed.

Literally, I make up every day with her on my mind and how I can add just a little more joy or value to her life that day.

Most people like to look for a partner who complements their life instead of one who improves it.

Like I said before, any significant relationship needs to add value to your life.

A woman can add value to a man's life by supporting him throughout life and all of his ventures. Make your husband feel like a superman. Believe in him and let him and the whole world know it. Even if his ideas sound weird, help and support him through it.

Here are some questions you can ask your loved one to ensure you are aware of how you can add value to his/her life:

- How do you know that I love you?
- What was the last really fun thing we did together?
- When you get hurt, how do you want me to respond?
- What can I do to add more happiness and joy in your life?
- What is the most important thing to you?
- How do you like to celebrate?
- How can I make you a better person?

Your mate needs to be able to make contributions in your life in significant ways.

Don't just focus on material things alone and forget about your spiritual life.

They're either enriching your spiritual growth toward God or pulling you away from God. It's one or the other. Relationships should always add to us and make us grow in our spiritual lives.

Are you adding value to your marriage? Do you even think about what you can do every day to keep this relationship growing?

Your purpose in a relationship is to give in the way your partner needs you to give. If you focus on yourself, then this can't and won't happen. Selfishness extinguishes flaming love.

Relationships work best when both partners put in equal effort to make things better for their own sakes.

Learning how to add value to your relationships simply revolves around what makes the other parties happy and the relationship better. Make plans to consistently add daily value to your spouse's life.

Discussion Questions

1. How do you plan to add value to your partner's life?

2. Why is it so important to add value to one another?

SECRET SIX
Boundaries

Day 21

Boundaries And Accountability

Scripture Meditation: "Your boundary lines mark out pleasant places for me. Indeed, my inheritance is something beautiful" (*Psalms 16:6, GW*).

My wife almost left me. Our marriage almost ended because I didn't honor our marriage boundaries.

I know first-hand the pain and disaster that awaits when boundaries are not set around the marriage. One of the greatest mistakes I made in the early days of our marriage is that I never instituted proper boundaries around our marriage, especially in the areas of generosity and dealing with the opposite sex.

Out of the kindness of my heart, I would give or loan people money without first discussing or consulting with my wife.

I was allowing people to get too close to my heart and kept it a secret from her. I've hurt my wife severely because of inappropriate relationships, conversations, texts, and meetings that violated the boundaries around our marriage.

There are certain levels of love, affection, and intimacy that are only reserved for your spouse. If you allow another to partake in any of those, you've invited an intruder into your marriage.

Whatever happens in Vegas stays in Vegas. It's the same with your marriage. There is certain information about your spouse or marriage that should never be discussed (unless it's a trusted counselor) with a third party—that list of third party includes your sister, best friend, parents, or coworker.

One of the greatest benefits that marriage brings to those who are in it is safety and comfort. Within that safety and comfort, you have someone who is your spouse, and they have your back—as they say in slang terms. In other words, someone will always be there for you during the good, the bad, and the ugly. With that security comes the responsibility to protect the relationship that you hold the most dear to you outside of the relationship you have with God.

In light of that, one of the ways that you will protect your marriage is through the setting of clear boundaries. Boundaries can be seen as the guardrails on the highway. If you notice, guardrails are set up at the point of the highway that if one drove that way, they would fall completely off the highway.

Picture your marriage as a highway to purpose and destiny. A part of your destiny is locked up within your spouse, and a part of your spouse's destiny is locked up within you. As you are driving on the highway together, those guardrails ensure that you do not veer off the highway of your destiny.

A marriage without boundaries is like a country without borders.

A country without borders can never be a strong and great nation. Marital boundaries protect you from affairs, emotional infidelity, putting the children first, overworking, using outside factors to compensate for inside issues, negative external influences, and the like.

Boundaries, just like guardrails, protect you from harm and danger. Many people run away from boundaries because they think it will imprison them and box them in. But the opposite is true—a marriage without boundaries often leads to emotional prison and divorce.

Accountability to God and to each other is necessary to keep your marital boundaries safe and strong. The truth is, you need each other to be the best version of yourselves as you can possibly be. Boundaries help you to achieve this.

Initially, if you're not used to having boundaries or creating them, it will seem a bit arduous. Keep going. As you continue, you will find that the boundaries become a part of your everyday life. Those boundaries will protect you, and you soon appreciate the benefits.

If you desire to have a strong, healthy and passionate marriage, you'll also need a strong boundary around it.

God wants your marriage to be resilient, fit, adoring, satisfying, harmonious, exciting and fulfilling. Remember, a marriage from heaven is about you out-kinding, out-loving, out-serving and adoring each other.

Take a look at the examples below for some boundaries that protect against infidelity, immoralities, and intruders:

- **Not a hint of immorality**. Neither of us should be alone with someone of the opposite sex without advance permission from the other. If possible, have a mutual friend of the same sex be present.

- **Absolute purity**. Confess sexual temptation early. People who make passes, offer dates, sex, or use suggestive language should be discussed. Make it safe to have the discussion with your spouse.

- **Keeping the marriage bed pure**. We focus solely on each other through eye contact and open communication. Come to a mutual agreement for any new activities or suggestions for the bedroom. Ensure that all suggestions and activities align with our beliefs.

- **Close the gates.** Refrain from all temptations to your five senses—taste, sight, touch, smell, and sound. Look away from the temptation of the eyes, close your ears to unholy sounds, don't taste or touch that which is not your spouse's. We will refrain from movies, books, or magazines with full or partial nudity or sexual innuendo.

Discussion Questions

1. What areas of your marriage are in need of boundaries?

2. Are there boundaries that have been outlined but we don't abide by?

3. Of the 4 boundaries listed, which one is the most crucial to implement in your marriage at this time?

Day 22

Dos and Don'ts

Scripture Meditation: "Simply say yes or no. Anything more than that comes from the evil one" (*Matthew 5:37, GW*).

For boundaries to work well, it must have rules of engagement, otherwise known as dos and don'ts.

What are the dos and don'ts in your relationship? Have you formed boundaries around them?

Remember that boundaries help to protect and preserve your relationship from hostile external forces.

Sadly, most people enter into marriage without knowing that boundaries are going to be the most pivotal aspects of marriage that if not discussed, lead to a myriad of problems. This is because boundaries are created from expectations.

Expectations are what it is you desire to see from your spouse, or how you would want them to react to a certain situation.

For example, Sean is a friendly guy who goes out often for lunch with his coworkers. After work one day, a female coworker asks Sean to join her for drinks after work. Sean's wife, Abbey, has an expectation of open communication, which would require Sean to communicate to her that his female coworker wants him to join her for drinks after work. Since Abbey's expectations were not clearly communicated to Sean, and no marital boundaries have been set, Sean refrained from sharing his plans of joining his coworker.

When Sean returned home at an abnormal hour, smelling of alcohol and having makeup on his shirt from innocently hugging his female coworker, an argument rang out and caused a rift between the married couple because Abbey felt deceived, and Sean felt untrusted.

Please notice the two major points of Sean and Abbey's dilemma: they had not **established** any **clear boundaries** and **expectations**.

The boundaries might have been held within one spouse, but it was not clearly set or communicated to the other. When this happens over and over again, it is an attack on the marriage, which weakens it. Once the marriage is weak enough, just the right amount of stress and pressure can cause the festering rift to become a split, and that split is an open door to infidelity, bitterness, unforgiveness, anger, and other emotions and actions that tear down a marriage.

In the beginning of the marriage, boundaries may be the last thing on your mind, but understand that once you say "I do" to your spouse, they are officially a part of you. No one wants to feel misunderstood or betrayed by the one that they have joined themselves with.

As your marriage continues, you will be better able to determine the healthy boundaries that will help establish your commitment and love for each other.

You can begin with something as simple as dos and don'ts.

Dos
- Consider your spouse's feelings.
- Listen to your spouse's thoughts.
- Keep an open mind.
- Communicate and set clear boundaries.

- Share all outside temptations with your spouse.
- Say "No" to all intruders.

Don'ts
- Take things personally.
- Use this time as an opportunity to manipulate, control.
- Underestimate the power of boundaries.
- Meet with the opposite sex alone or without your spouse's consent or involvement.
- Keep secrets.
- Value the opinions of others above that of your mate.

The easiest way to understand setting boundaries within your marriage is to step outside of yourself and consider the thoughts and feelings of your spouse.

When you are not able to communicate clearly without omitting information, hiding information, or having to tell 'white lies,' that is an immediate ground for you to reveal to your spouse the situation at hand. No one likes to feel like they are being used or mistreated. These sentiments appear and permeate when a spouse is unable to or refuses to speak truthfully and honestly.

Discussion Questions

1. What boundaries can you set in place that will help and protect your relationship?

2. Are there any boundaries that haven't been discussed but need to be?

3. What can I do to cultivate an atmosphere conducive to open and honest communication?

Day 23

The Trust Factor

Scripture Meditation: "I trust your love, and I feel like celebrating because you rescued me" (Psalms 13:5, CEV).

The best marriages are built upon a foundation of good friendship and trust. Before anything romantic happens, friendship needs to be present. Without trust, there is no relationship. It's impossible to be intimate with someone you don't trust.

Boundaries help to build trust in your relationship. Your spouse will trust you more when they know that you abide by the boundaries of your marriage.

Boundaries are a GOOD thing because they help us to stay safe and healthy in different situations. There are visible and invisible, spoken and unspoken boundaries for nearly every part of our lives, including our marriage.

Contrary to what you may believe, your spouse is more in tune with you than you know. If you are hiding or withholding information, they know. This is how intimacy is hindered within a relationship.

Say, for instance, you are withholding information with the thought that you want to spare your spouse hurt or pain; that will further hurt them than you know.

As you withhold that information, your spouse can sense your inability to be free with them. In turn, as a means of self-preservation, they will begin to withhold their love and affection from you too.

This scenario often plays out when partners carry emotional baggage into the relationship.

In order to spare the other person hurt or pain, you withhold information or yourself, and in turn, your partner will do the same.

What your spouse doesn't know will hurt them. As a matter of fact, it will diminish the trust factor within the relationship. Without trust, there is no relationship. Your spouse needs to know your heart, your thoughts, and your perspective. And you must allow your spouse the same right. Closing parts of yourself off from your spouse can build a barrier against intimacy and trust.

Be a safe place. Every husband needs to be his wife's refuge and vice versa. Your best friend is the person you call when something great or terrible happens.

When trust has been broken

Restoring *trust* takes time. It's a process that requires both an accurate understanding and an appropriate application of the principle of *forgiveness*. But you can't begin to move in this direction until you know what the words *trust* and *forgiveness* really mean.

Trust is something that has to be earned. Trust can be broken fairly quickly, but the rebuilding process can be lengthy and tedious. This is especially true where the offenses in question were unusually hurtful, or if they've been repeated numerous times.

When you've been hurt and wounded, it's hard to trust again unless you can see concrete evidence that things are going to be different in the future. But learn to forgive and support the offending spouse as they go through their process of healing, repair, and restoration.
Please don't make it too hard for them. The offending spouse is probably hurting more than you realize, so your prayer, love, and care will go a long way to help

them overcome the shame and guilt eating them up for their breach of your family covenant.

Many times, when boundaries are respected, it's easier to maintain trust in the marriage.

To help to rebuild trust, the offending spouse should:

1. *Accept personal responsibility for their actions.*
2. *Seek the forgiveness of God.*
3. *Seek the forgiveness of their wounded spouse.*
4. *Avoid playing the blame game.*
5. *Forgive themselves and start the healing process.*
6. *Understand that the wounded spouse needs time to grief and process the pain without undue pressure.*
7. *Cut off completely and permanently any outside party that participated in the situation where trust was lost.*
8. *Have a commitment to counseling/therapy.*
9. *Make a determination to come up with a precise and definitive plan designed to prevent further offenses.*
10. *Understand that trust might never be restored in the marriage, but you have a huge part to play in rebuilding it.*

Discussion Questions

1. What must you do to maintain trust in your marriage?

2. Why is it difficult to rebuild trust?

Day 24

Protecting Your Marriage From Intruders

Scripture Meditation: "That is why a man will leave his father and mother and will be united with his wife, and they will become one flesh" (*Genesis 2:24, GW*).

When God created marriage, He created foundational principles for it to be guided and guarded. One of those principles is boundaries. It is stated in the Scripture above. Once we are married, we are no longer two but one.

God created marriage to produce the deepest intimacy and bonding possible in a human relationship.

There are many unknowing couples whose relationship has been surrendered to the opinions and whims of others because boundaries were not in place. **If you don't set boundaries for your marriage, other people will do it for you.** There is no guarantee that the boundaries others set will be beneficial to you either.

Most often than not, people push the boundaries of you and your relationship to see what it will take before they get what they want.

It must be said that boundaries are not the time in which you allow your personal fears, failures, control issues, and the like take over. Again, boundaries are a form of protection and preservation from the outside influences that have the ability to influence it in a negative way.

Who are marriage intruders?

Marriage intruders are external people that try to violate your marriage boundaries and covenant.

A marriage from heaven is between two people (not three or more) God put together to do life together.

You must protect your marriage from intruders. Some intruders are those who you love and care the most about. Though their thoughts and motives might be good and pure, their actions can damage and destroy your marriage. Before you know it, they could split you and your spouse.

Boundaries should be made mutually, meaning that both parties agree to the boundaries set.

No two individuals are the same. Your perspective may be different from your spouse's, but for the mutual benefit of preserving the relationship, boundaries must be met.

Protect your marriage from intruders. One of the most effective ways is to set boundaries.

How To Set Boundaries:

1. State what you think the boundaries should be.

2. Allow your partner to state what they think the boundaries should be.

3. Then come to a mutual agreement or meet in the middle. You will find that when the two of you are on the same page, it makes for an ideal situation.

Always remember that in order for your spouse to feel comfortable and be open and honest, you must create an atmosphere that is conducive for honesty through your words, behavior, anger management, attitude, and emotional maturity.

As husband and wife, we should be the first to protect each other's reputations. We should never allow our family, friends, or anyone for that matter to speak negatively about our spouse. Marriage is between two people and not a crowd. The moment you allow an intruder into your marriage, you've already weakened its borders.

Don't keep secrets from each other. Be a team — one team. Unless we are planning a surprise party for our spouse, we have no business keeping any secrets from him/her. Marriage is for lovers!

Discussion Questions

1. Who are the intruders trying to gain access to your marriage?

2. What are you going to do, beginning today, to stop the intruders?

3. How do you plan to gain the trust of your mate?

SECRET SEVEN
Money

Day 25

Creating Financial Intimacy

Scripture Meditation: "A meal is made for laughter, and wine makes life pleasant, but money is the answer for everything" (*Ecclesiastes 10:19, GW*).

I heard one FBI agent say, "If you are looking for a fugitive, 'follow the money.'" The direction of the flow of money will always lead to the fugitive. It's the same with love and marriage. *If he/she is not investing money in you, it's because their heart is not into you.* For example, men like to work and provide. So, if a man is working but not spending money on his wife and home, we bet you 9 out of 10, his heart is shifted away from the relationship.

Temika was in love when she dated Jerome for three years and then married another four years. Their marriage was rocky, and she met with me (Uyi) for a counseling session to try to save it. After a few questions, it became clear that Jerome hasn't paid a single bill since they had been together. He had worked the whole time but came up with excuses why he can't or shouldn't pay any bill in the house. She said she thought he was saving his money for their future together but only to realize that he had been spending his money on strippers, drinking, and taking exotic trips with other females.

It was clear to me that Temika and Jerome, though married, had no financial intimacy. They shared a house and a bed but not their money. When Jerome's heart shifted away from his marriage, he turned to strippers, drinking, and riotous living.

I wished I could tell you of a happy ending to this story, but unfortunately, they broke up and divorced.

Two shall become one. That is not only emotionally, spiritually, and sexually but also financially as well.

In over a decade of counseling couples, we've often seen that financial intimacy is one of the most difficult things for couples to form.

People marry for emotional, sexual, and physical reasons, but not a lot marry for financial considerations. Talking about money is usually a very touchy subject for many couples. Financial intimacy? Many people are shocked by this. Getting naked with your finances?

If you can be naked with your body, why can't you be naked with your finances or money?

Joining bank accounts with your spouse can be one of the most petrifying aspects of a new relationship for some partners. Some consider it more scary than meeting the in-laws!

In our fore fathers' generations, it was a norm for couples to marry young. They would then move in together, start a family, get new jobs and open a joint checking account. They grew together in love and finances as they went through life together.

Nowadays, you are most already financially set before marriage. Now, you're married and have to surrender some of your financial freedom. You've been used to leading and managing your finances all by yourself; it's hard to now open it to the scrutiny and discretion of another. Yet, that is one of the most fun and healthy parts of marriage—doing life and finances together.

We thank God that when it comes to money and finances, we have been very strong. We share our money together. We have one main business account where our business income go into, and we pay ourselves and business-related bills from that single business joint account.

We also have individual accounts for our own individual spending and discretion. This is key!

We challenge couples to have a joint bank account, joint savings account, and also individual bank accounts as well.

Having individual bank accounts will save your marriage from financial arguments and fights. You need to be able to spend some money without the oversight and scrutiny of your spouse.

For example, *Faith* doesn't need to consult with *Uyi* to buy a new pair of shoes or a burger. She can easily buy that from her personal account. But if she wants to buy a new vehicle or furniture, that is a major project and should come from our joint account after due consultation.

That is how we manage the finances in our home and relationship, and it's been working very well. Also, we don't hide money from each other. We are not selfish or stingy when it comes to our finances. We both partake of every single dollar that comes into the family.

We have this big idea that if we can share our lives and bodies together, so does our finances.

We want you to get financially intimate. Deal with your fears and trust issues. Speak to a financial counselor if you need to. Financial intimacy is a must if you want to experience a marriage from heaven.

Money problems are one of the top three leading causes of divorce in America and all over the world. According to a recent survey, 42% of couples do not talk about money before they are married. Bad money habits will cripple and burn out the love and sparks in a relationship faster than anything you can think about. It's a plus for you both to educate yourself about money. Discover and reveal your Money Personalities.

Discussion Questions

1. How would you describe the level of financial intimacy in your marriage?

2. Do you trust your spouse with finances?

3. What steps can you both take to become more financially intimate?

Day 26

Financial Health

Scripture Meditation: "Beloved, I pray that you may prosper in all things and be in health, just as your soul prospers" (3 *John* 2, *NKJV*).

Money issues are one of the top three reasons that most relationships and marriages fail. One relationship expert says that money talk before marriage is the most important conversation to have before you say "I do."

So, let's talk about money. Before we do, we want to remind you again that God's idea for your marriage is one where you both serve one another. Serving one another includes serving them with your finances.

How can you say you love your spouse when you hide your money and finances from them?

You shouldn't hide or withhold anything from your spouse. Financial healthiness is a prerequisite for building a strong, healthy and passionate marriage.

You are married; stop dating your money.

Bad spending habits can ruin a loving relationship faster than anything you think. Now, here is the catch: to be truly financially healthy, you have to first be healthy in your soul. You have to be healthy so your money can be healthy.

Over the years, we've discovered that a lot of people have an unhealthy relationship with money. It's like they are dating their money, and it's hard for them to share with anyone else.

Some even try to use money to fill a void in their lives. *How you handle money shows something about your emotional health.*

If you are an impulsive spender, it could mean that you are trying to use the purchase of new things to hide or mask a pain, trauma, hurt, or abuse in your life. More money can never take the pain away, and new things cannot substitute for the need for healing and/or deliverance in your life.

Also, if you and your potential partner are selfish with money, then I can guarantee that you both will be selfish in affection as well. *A financially selfish and stingy person is a person that will be selfish with their love and emotions.*

We will say it another way: a person that is selfish with money will also be selfish with their love and will withhold their feelings and emotions from you.

You need to understand how you look at and deal with money individually and together as a team. Knowing this information now will save you lots of problems in your marriage. Another mistake many couples make about money is spending more money on their wedding than they can afford. They plan financially for their wedding but not their marriage. And then months and years into the marriage, they are still busy paying off debts and the credit cards they spent to impress people on their wedding day.

Here's my advice on this: plan a wedding you can pay for with cash.

Here are some Money conversation starting questions:

- Who is better at money between the two of us?
- Who is the more disciplined spender?
- Individual bank accounts or joint accounts?
- Can our current earnings support the standard of living we want for ourselves and future children?

- How much do we need to start saving toward our future?
- What financial sacrifices do we need to start making now?
- How do you envision financing your children's college education or your retirement?
- Do any of your dreams need to be included in your financial plans?
- What major adventures or fantasies do you have that we need to plan for financially?

Discussion Questions

1. How are we doing in our financial health?

2. Do you see any streak of financial selfishness in the marriage?

Day 27

Budgeting

Scripture Meditation: "Suppose you want to build a tower. You would first sit down and figure out what it costs. Then you would see if you have enough money to finish it. Otherwise, if you lay a foundation and can't finish the building, everyone who watches will make fun of you. They'll say, 'This person started to build but couldn't finish the job'" (*Luke 14: 28–30*).

Here is one of the most difficult things for married couples to do—budgeting. This is one of the most common entrance points for arguments and fights within a relationship.

Money is such a touchy thing for couples to talk about without fighting. It is hard to move from the mindset of caring for your own financial needs to balancing the needs of your spouse with your own. As you sit down to plan out your budget with your spouse, spend time together talking. Be free to express yourself and your needs very clearly. Here is a guide to help you with your budgeting:

a. Know What You Both Bring In
Here is the first thing to do. Determine how much you both bring in each month to the family. Calculate your gross incomes, and then take out your taxes and tithe of ten percent to your local church. When you determine your net, that is what you will be working with.

b. Determine Your Household Needs
Then add up your household needs. This would include things such as rent or mortgage, utility payments, groceries, car payments, and debt payments.

c. Find Ways To Save
Always find ways to save money. The more money you have to save or spend in your marriage, the less stress you'll have to deal with in your relationship. There is wiggle room to negotiate your bills and make some savings. You can save money by buying a less expensive car, eating out, cutting back on groceries, renting a smaller place. These obligations need to be met before either of you begin to budget in your luxury items.

c. Create Long-Term Goals

It is important to set goals that you can work on as a couple. Goal setting also helps to bring couples closer to each other. These long-term goals should be part of your financial plan.

Don't be short-sighted. Dream, plan, and budget for long-term goals. The plan can help you determine how soon you can buy a house or when to start a family.

Every couple should have a credible plan for their future.

d. Plan For Retirement

It can also help you to plan for retirement or your dream vacation. When you have specific goals that you are working toward each month, it can make sticking to a budget easier. If you are just limiting spending and saving without a goal in mind, it is easier to justify overspending on a regular basis.

Some good beginning goals are to get out of debt and to begin to save for a down payment for your home. You should also make saving for retirement an important part of your financial plan.

e. Pay Off The Debts

Create a plan to pay off your debt. List your debts from highest interest rate to lowest and start paying them off one at a time. Make clear savings goals and determine when you want to hit each of the financial milestones as a couple. A clear plan will help you be ready to buy a home or move onto the next step. Be sure to include retirement as part of this planning process.

f. Address Your Individual Needs
Once you have determined your household needs, you can begin to talk about individual needs and wants.

We told you earlier that we have a joint bank account and also individual bank accounts. You may want to set up an allowance for each of you to spend on your wants without being accountable to the other person.
- Listen to your partner to understand what is important to them.
- Make sure that each of you has money to spend on the things that are most important to you.
- As long as each partner is sticking to the set agreed amount, there is no reason to argue or fight about how that money is spent.

It can help to choose good financial software that you can sync with your phones.

As you get better at following your budget, these meetings can be shorter and just as effective. Budgeting is like boundaries. It helps to protect and preserve couples from falling off the guardrails of life.

Don't allow personal greed pollute your marriage. Plan for the future together. Be prepared for it.

When finances are kept separate, couples can lose some of the intimacy of shared goals.

Many spouses have ideas for the future, and taking part in them together makes them more meaningful. It brings the couple closer.

Discussion Questions

1. Do you have a family budget?

2. What are some of your long-term goals?

3. Where do you see your marriage five years from now?

Day 28
The Power Of Generosity

Scripture Meditation: "For where your treasure is, there will be also your heart" (*Matthew 6:21, KJV*).

We learned early on that generosity was key to a happy and satisfying marriage. Generosity and considerate behaviors can go a long way toward nurturing a great marriage. Nothing changes a heart like habitual generosity.

Couples who try to out-give one another with love and material substance tend to live happier fulfilling lives. Instead of wondering if he/she will ever load the dishwasher right, do something you know your spouse will appreciate.

Be prepared: they may not throw you a Las Vegas size parade because you did it. Remember, you didn't do it for their applause. You serve because you love your spouse; so don't get caught up in the "what's in it for me" trap.

God created us to be generous beings. We live to give and give to live.

We care about where we are invested.

If you continue a pattern of being more generous and thoughtful toward your spouse, they'll eventually say or do something as a response. They might hold their comments back at first because they don't know if this trend will stick. They may be waiting to see if this generosity is a gimmick or a set of new, positive habits.

When they see that you are genuine and consistent with your efforts over time, your message will be clear. Let those selfish thoughts pass by, and keep doing loving things for your spouse.

We've said over and over again that **selfishness** is one of the leading causes of many failed marriages. The opposite of selfishness is generosity. Be a generous lover.

Here's another secret about making an effort like this: Feelings follow actions. In other words, you may not feel appreciated at first when you do these generous acts. If you don't feel appreciated at first, you may really wonder if all your efforts are in vain. Keep going anyway. The more you act with generosity, the more you'll naturally feel generous and loving toward your spouse.

A healthy marriage includes generosity, openness, honest conversation, and the enjoyment of shared interests.

Think of new ways on how you can be more generous to your mate. Shower them with gifts and kindness. You will be surprised how they respond to you in love.

As discussed in an earlier chapter, one of the primary love languages of women is *receiving gifts*. To a woman, each gift has an equal value. Many men don't realize that to women, the little things are as important as the large gifts.

Gifts from the heart tend to mean more to women than large gifts money can buy.

There's no amount of money a man can spend on a woman that can replace the sense of security and exclusivity she needs in that relationship. Make her feel secure in you, and she'll lower her guard and receive you into her heart!

Also remember to have fun and be creative. Having fun in marriage dramatically improves your relationship. In fact, one of the danger signs in a marriage is when a husband and wife stop having fun together. Husbands and wives need to enter into each other's worlds and spend time laughing, playing, and enjoying each other's company.

Discussion Questions

1. Why is generosity important in marriage?

2. How do you plan to be more generous toward your spouse?

3. Do you feel appreciated in your relationship?

SECRET EIGHT

Visioneering

Day 29

Creating A Vision For Your Marriage

Scripture Meditation: "Where there is no vision, the people cast off restraint; But he that keepeth the law, happy is he" (*Proverbs 29:18, ASV*).

Patrick and Susan fight all the time. Their fifteen years of marriage was in shambles and ready to end. They could hardly agree on anything without arguing. They got scheduled for a marriage session.

One of the very first questions I asked them was: "What is the vision for your marriage?"

They looked at each other, gazed at me and looked at each other again before nodding their heads in disbelief.

"Well, hmmnn …" his voice shaking. "We don't have any," he responded.

I went on to teach them about the importance of visioneering and having a compelling visualization for their marriage.

Couples who have nothing to fight together for often fight against each other.

I regularly cast a vision for our marriage. My wife and I create time to sit, write, and fantasize about the future together. It's a good bonding time for us.

It also helps us to focus on what is important in our marriage and where we are headed together.

The Bible says, "Then the Lord answered me and said: 'Write the vision and make it plain on tablets, That he may run who reads it'" (*Habakkuk 2:2*).

It was in one of those visioneering sessions that we wrote the basic outline for this book. *Marriage From Heaven,* is one of the major visions for our lives—*to help couples build strong, healthy and passionate marriages.*

Visioneering is the act of a couple coming together, dreaming, and planning for the future. Vision is needed in all areas of marriage—faith, family, finance, fun, etc.

Andy Stanley writes, "Vision is the tension between what is and what ought to be."

A couple that dreams together stays together. We encourage you to regularly create time out of your busy schedules to pray, plan, and strategize together toward the future. This is healthy for your marriage.

I (Uyi) did not come from my mother's womb as a natural visionary. As a child, I rarely planned beyond the next day. I never saw the power of visioneering until much later in life.

When I got hold of the power of vision, I knew that to be successful in life, whether in business, sport, or marriage, you'll have to create a vision. A vision is like a compass to a destination. One of the first things we did even before I got married to my beautiful wife (Faith) was to cast a clear vision for our marriage. I remember sitting down on the bare carpet in her apartment in Arlington, Texas, pouring my heart on the vision I see for our marriage.

My vision included a conflict-free marriage, pastoring a great church together, debt-free lifestyle, entrepreneurship, and traveling the world for fun and in preaching the gospel. I even told her if she married me, I would retire her at age thirty and take her all around the world.

Listen to me; at the time I was sharing this wonderful vision for marriage with my wife, I was struggling financially; I didn't have a job, regular income, or money in the bank. Yet I believed in the power of vision. Like we told you in Chapter one, when God is in the midst and center of your marriage, you both can accomplish great feats together that will mesmerize all around you.

By the grace of God, in over thirteen years of marriage (at the time of this writing), we've never had a fight, except a few heated exchanges. This is because physical and verbal fights were never in our marriage vision.

Could it be that the both of you can't seem to stop fighting because you never had a clear vision for your marriage?

Decide in advance how you want your marriage to be and work together to that destination.

We tell couples all the time that they have to have a God-inspired vision for their marriage. If God has a purpose for your marriage — and I believe He does —

then vision is letting God reveal to you what that purpose is. It's asking, "God, why did You put us together?" and listening for the answer.

A marriage from heaven must contain a heavenly-inspired vision for that marriage as well. Why is a vision for your marriage so important?

Here are five reasons:

a. Purpose is revealed
A purpose mate is the one that God yoked up with you in marriage before you were born. A vibrant vision helps you to realize that your spouse is not just someone to live with but also your purpose mate. When God coded your purpose, He also coded the right spouse for you. Hopefully, you didn't marry your spouse just because they were cute or attractive. A successful marriage depends on: (1) marrying your purpose mate; (2) finding the right person; and (3) being the right person.

We have counseled countless unfilled and frustrated spouses who did not marry their purpose mate because they never had a vision for their marriage.

b. Vision brings clarity
It helps to bring a perspective to why God put you together. It's impossible to know if you're successful if you don't know what it is you're trying to

accomplish. Confusion is the opposite of clarity, and God never creates anything to operate in confusion. God wants to operate in light. He will speak to us and give us clarity if we'll let him.

c. Vision gives Energy and passion
If you don't know the vision for your life and marriage, it's hard to get excited about it. Once you identify a vision, both of you will pursue it with enormous energy.

When God gives us a desire, He equips us to pursue it. Faith and I love what we do. We wake up every day excited and elated to spend time together in God's presence and in using our skills and talents to help marriages succeed.

d. Vision protects your marriage
One of the best decisions we ever made in our marriage was to define it from the very beginning.

The Bible says that without vision, people cast off restraint. They fall into sin. People without vision are vulnerable to negative guidance and all kinds of trouble. Rather than living your life attempting not to fail or struggling not to do bad things, with a vision, you'll live doing good things.

That's a huge psychological difference.

e. Vision brings unity
Couples tend to fight when they don't see eye-to-eye. Not having a clear vision opens the door to competing visions and ideas for the marriage that brings disunity and confrontation. Two people cannot walk together unless they're in agreement. It is easy to fail in marriage when a husband and wife are divided. Rather than both of you having your own way of looking at things, a single vision for your marriage means you both have the same focus and are on the same page.

Discussion Questions:

1. What is the vision for your marriage?

2. What united the both of you together in marriage in the beginning? Can you share with each other?

Day 30

Two Becoming One

Scripture Meditation: "And said, 'For this reason a man shall leave his father and mother and be joined to his wife, and the two shall become one flesh'? ⁶ So then, they are no longer two but one flesh. Therefore what God has joined together, let not man separate" (*Matthew 19:5–6, NKJV*).

Two becoming one doesn't happen overnight. It takes time, effort, and work to really become one. They say that Rome wasn't built in a day—the same with strong and healthy marriages. A marriage from heaven happens gradually as the husband and wife intentionally work on becoming one. We strongly recommend that you have a vision retreat with your spouse.

Every three months, go somewhere far or near to reconnect and refocus on each other and your marriage. A vision retreat will help you resolve issues and find agreement. Having the same vision keeps you and your spouse united.

God desires that every couple have a marriage from heaven. This happens to the extent that couples give and receive grace and truth in their relationship and really strive to become one. We hope you'll consider taking a vision retreat with your spouse. I've seen it change marriages forever.

Power Of Prayer

Couples that pray together stay longer together. One of the most fascinating things about praying together is that prayer bonds your heart and mind like nothing else in the world. Spending time together in God's presence brings about an everlasting change. Couples should develop a habit of praying for each other.

Paul prayed for the Philippians in chapter 1, verses 9 and 10. He writes: *This is my prayer; that your love may abound more and more in knowledge and depth of insight, so that you may be able to discern what is best and may be pure and blameless until the day of Christ.*

We've found this prayer to be a beautiful expression of what we want to experience in our marriage. We often encourage other couples to do the same.

Do fun things together. Take a walk, read a book, or see a movie. Prioritize quality times together. Sometimes, turn off the phone and pour into each other and make your spouse feel special.

Pour your time and abilities into serving your spouse, and your spouse will be drawn back to you. Continually investing in each other helps you stay passionate about each other. Remember that God's ultimate goal is for the both of you to become as one flesh. Don't stop developing until you achieve that goal.

Discussion Questions:

1. In what specific ways can you both work to become one?

2. What fun things can you add to your marriage?

3. When is your next couple's retreat?

Day 31

Dealing With Compatibility Issues

Scripture Meditation: "Can two walk together, unless they are agreed?" (*Amos 3:3, NKJV*).

When it comes to compatibility, my wife and I couldn't be more different. For example, she loves to clean and organize the house. She likes to see the clothes hung in the right places, and the shoes in the shoe closet. I am the opposite. I am not as clean and organized like her. I tend to find myself throwing my clothes into the closet instead of hanging them and leaving my shoes and socks out in the living room instead of the shoe closet.

When dating, people usually choose their opposites. For many couples, their differences can become a source of frustration and conflict. When you learn that your differences actually supply what you're lacking, marriage becomes a healing journey.

Visioneering helped us to see and strengthen the areas of our marriage where we needed to improve our compatibility.

Compatibility issues are one of the reasons why many marriages fail. People get high in love and infatuations and jump into marriage without checking to see if they were even compatible in the first place.

Marriage compatibility should be considered before you get into a serious relationship. Don't wait until you are emotionally and physically involved before you start logically evaluating the wisdom of such a union.

While it's true that you need someone different to complement you and your personality, research findings are highly consistent that the most stable marriages are those involving two people with many similarities. Society says that opposite attracts. Though this is true in many instances, in marriage, too much of the opposite repels.

To experience a marriage from heaven, the both of you will have to be compatible.

WHAT IS COMPATIBILITY?

Webster defines compatibility as "the capability to live together in harmony." That is key—living in harmony. Marriage is pointless if it doesn't add joy, peace, and harmony in your life. A quick search on Google on the word 'Compatible' brings up this result: "(of two things) able to exist or occur together without conflict."

You'll have a much stronger relationship when the both of you share common values and attributes.

You don't have to be 100 percent compatible in order to make a long-term relationship work. But there are a few areas that you'll find it beneficial to be compatible.

The greater the compatibility you share with your partner, the easier and less stressful your relationship will be. Here are five areas of compatibility I'd like for you to assess:

a. Spiritual Compatibility

Having a relationship with Jesus is essential to developing a strong marriage character. A strong character is crucial to having a strong, healthy and passionate love and married life.

Continue to develop your spiritual compatibility by pursuing God together. If you allow your spouse to be on fire for God while you slack in the same efforts, you are bringing spiritual incompatibility to the relationship.

b.   Values and Moral Compatibility

Astoundingly, you both can be very strong Christians and yet have huge differences when it comes to how you live out your faith in daily life. Your values have to align to be harmonious in marriage. They often say that opposites attract. It's mostly false in marriage and relationship building. It is pointless to date or marry someone who is so fundamentally different from you in terms of values and morals. Like the Bible says, light and darkness cannot co-exist. A good example: if you believe strongly in monogamy, and the person you're married to believes in having numerous sexual partners, that would equal incompatibility.

c.   Life Dreams and Vision Compatibility

For the both of you to have a loving and happy relationship together, your life dreams and core visions must align.

You both need to have similar worldviews and goals in life. It doesn't need to be the same goals, dreams, and visions, but not too far apart that you both can't see eye to eye on the future destination of your relationship.

d. Financial Compatibility

It is common in many marriages where one of the spouses is better with money than the other. Sometimes, this friction causes lots of problem in the marriage. Money issues and differences in financial priorities is the leading cause of divorce and relationship breakups in America. For your marriage to be strong and healthy, you'll need to develop a common financial strength, goals, and togetherness. We encourage couples to learn to develop similar financial taste and spending habits. Have compatible financial goals for your marriage and family.

Discussion Questions:

1. What areas of your marriage would you need to be more compatible?

2. What are some of the short-term vision for your marriage?

3. What are some of the long-term vision for your marriage?

Day 32

The Big Picture

Scripture Meditation: "Do two walk together unless they have agreed to do so?" (*Amos 3:3*).

"Did God put you together?" That was the question I asked a couple who came to me for a marital counseling session last year. Your guess is as good as mine.
"Yes!" They said almost in a chorus.
But they were not ready for my next question. "Why did He put you together?"
Here comes the blank stare.

They believe that God put them together but don't know why. We believe God made us for each other, but many of us have no idea why. This is always because they have not been visioneering.

Visioneering paints the big picture of God for your lives and marriage. Helping couples discover God's purpose for their marriage is one of the things my husband and I are passionate about. It can absolutely transform your relationship.

We were made for relationships. God wants us to have successful relationships. On the other hand, the devil wants to destroy relationships by either unraveling us from God or separating us from each other—especially from our spouse. Satan is always trying to divide and conquer.

We see in the Bible, in Genesis, with Adam and Eve. God put them in a perfect paradise where they were experiencing marriage from heaven, but Satan lied and convinced them that God was evil. He divided Adam and Eve from God. He does this to couples today in so many different ways. Don't let the devil lie to you concerning your spouse. When you hear voices in your head that are antagonistic to the big picture of your marriage, you need to reject those thoughts quickly.

You need to know that God wants you to have a big picture for your marriage. A big picture is a vision of your future. Having a passionate marriage is a goal that should be in your big picture.

A marriage from heaven is one that is full of passion and holy lust for each other.

A big picture helps you and your spouse to handle conflicts in a much easier fashion.

My husband and I always remind ourselves of the big picture of our marriage. It helps us avoid unnecessary arguments, petty fights, and selfishness that kill other marriages.

Please hear us again: it's time for you and your spouse to determine your big picture and start working toward it.

Discussion Questions:

1. When was the last time you did something intentional for your spouse?

2. What are you doing today toward the big picture of your marriage?

3. What would you stop doing because it is against the big picture of your marriage?

SECRET NINE
Family Dynamics

Day 33

Spiritual Forces At Work

Scripture Meditation: "For the weapons of our warfare are not carnal but mighty in God for pulling down strongholds, ⁵ casting down arguments and every high thing that exalts itself against the knowledge of God, bringing every thought into captivity to the obedience of Christ" (*2 Corinthians 10:4–5, NKJV*).

Marriage is spiritual. It is the greatest invention God ever created. The idea of bringing two very different people together to be one is beyond this life. Only God can do this and sustain it.

Marriage is the only institution created by God that will never be destroyed. The scripture tells us that the whole earth is going to be destroyed one day by fire—all that is in eschatology, which is not the scope of this book, but so you know how important the marriage union is to God and His plan for mankind. Jesus is coming back again to the earth, the Bible tells us.

Why is He coming back? Jesus is coming back to come and get His bride (the church) so the two can be forever.

Here is what the scripture says: "A husband should love his wife as much as Christ loved the church and gave his life for it. He made the church holy by the power of his word, and he made it pure by washing it with water. Christ did this, so that he would have a glorious and holy church, without faults or spots or wrinkles or any other flaws" (*Ephesians 5:25–27, CEV*).

The devil knows how important marriage is to God and humans, and so he fights it with everything he's got. Your marriage might be under a spiritual attack right now, and you don't even know it.

The enemy of your marriage is not your spouse.

Satanic forces loathe Christian marriages. You need to be aware of that so you can fortify yourself and your marriage. The real enemy of your marriage is the devil — spiritual forces you cannot see.

Nothing gives the devil greater joy than divorces.

Every divorce or bad marriage is viewed as a win in hell. You'll have to fight and protect your marital territory.

Spiritual Warfare In Marriage

Have you ever felt frustrated, miserable, lonely, upset, or angry with your spouse? The easy answer is "Yes!" But then the next question is, "Why did you get so upset?" It is easy to blame your spouse. But the truth is that the devil probably influenced your disgust for your spouse. The primary goal of Satan is to bring and facilitate discord between you and your partner.

Spiritual warfare is real in marriages. Sometimes, when you feel like there's no connection happening between you and your partner, you feel as though you're sleeping with the enemy. You lose the desire for sexual intimacy. The attraction seems to have evaporated into thin air. All these are signs of spiritual warfare.

The *first strategy* in spiritual warfare is to identify your enemy.

The *second strategy* is to formulate a strategy against the enemy causing problems in your marriage.

The *third strategy* is to fight together.

Stop pointing fingers at each other. As long as you focus on fighting each other or blaming yourself, your marriage will continue to slide into further misery and despair with each failed request for intimacy, each unmet expectation, each day spent hopelessly wishing your spouse would change.

But you can fight united and defeat the real enemy of your marriage—Satan and his kingdom.

Sure, you need to learn to work together as a unit, communicate better, pray together, serve one another, and develop financial intimacy and every principle of marriage we have been teaching in this book.

You need to learn how to forgive. Your spouse needs to do the same.

Praying for your Marriage

Spiritual warfare in your marriage is not about praying for God to whip your spouse into shape because they have failed you! It's really not much about your spouse at all. It's about clearing the way for God to do the work He wants to do in both of you.

Applying spiritual warfare principles to your troubled marriage is not for the faint of heart! Remember, the enemy cares so much about your marriage because he knows how much destruction a troubled marriage can bring and how much damage a healthy, godly marriage can do to his kingdom of darkness.

Have you been fighting your spouse? Are you ready to join forces to fight the true enemy of your marriage? I'd love to hear from you if this perspective is helpful. Please let me know in the comments below.

1. Pray against the plans of the devil for your marriage.
2. Pray for spiritual growth in your marriage.
3. Bind up the strongman that was sent against your marriage.
4. Declare peace, joy, and harmony in your marriage.
5. Pray for humility and the guidance of the Holy Spirit.
6. Pray against any temptations sent to your marriage.
7. Pray for emotional health, intimacy, and fidelity.
8. Pray for your sex life.
9. Declare the blessings and favor of God on your marriage.
10. Pray for your spouse to fulfill the will of God for their lives.

Discussion Question

1. How do you plan to combat the spiritual forces working against your marriage?

2. Name some of the prayer strategies you will use against Satan and his kingdom.

3. Why is it vital that both couples fight together during spiritual warfare?

Day 34

Raising Godly Children

Scripture Meditation: "Children are a blessing and a gift from the Lord" (*Psalms 127:3, CEV*).

"Zoe, it's time for bed!" You can hear my wife's voice across the hallway. Our children have come to realize that to be the code of a time of worship, scripture reading, and prayer before bed.

I honestly give all the credit to my wife for helping us raise godly kids. All three of our children love the Lord.

We've come to understand that one of the divine reasons for our marriage is to raise godly children. God cares about the continuation of His kingdom here on earth. That was on His mind when He brought Adam and Eve together.

In fact, here is what the scriptures say: "God gave them his blessing and said: Have a lot of children! Fill the earth with people and bring it under your control. Rule over the fish in the ocean, the birds in the sky, and every animal on the earth" (*Genesis 1:28, CEV*).

Now, we understand that some of you might decide not to have children or are unable to have children. We are not trying to make you feel guilty about not having children. As a matter of fact, you can skip this section and go over to Day 35.

So, today, we want to encourage you to raise your children in the godliest way possible. Model a marriage from heaven for them to see that marriage still works.

Your marriage should precede your children in priority. Don't put the children before your spouse. Happiness and security in a marriage are essential for raising healthy, responsible children. When your child sees that you are happy and secure, it makes them happy and secure.

Jimmy Evans wrote, "Children can pick up tension in your relationship, even if you're not fighting in front of them. They internalize that tension, which can damage their physical health and their psychological well-being. Get your marriage on track first."

Try not to fight or argue when your children are around. In the society, children are usually viewed as a burden and hindrance to happiness.

However, when properly prepared for and trained, God can use your children to bless you with future happiness and support. Allow your children to see the way you love each other, serve each other, and affirm one another.

Parents must agree on the standards they want their children to uphold and then design wise guidelines for them to follow in order to keep those standards.

Both parents must be living examples of the behavior they want in their children and realize that discipline is not a periodic action but a growing relationship.

Don't allow the society to raise and train your children for you. Train them in the ways of the Lord. That includes engaging in regular prayer time with them, Bible reading, and taking them with you to church.

Don't be afraid to disciple your kids. The Lord trusted them to you to help mold their character into kingdom men and women. This means you must discipline in the same ways. You both need to show the same amount of affection and concern. Agree before time your parenting style and be unified in it.

Don't put the pressure on yourself trying to be perfect parents. You may encounter challenges along the way, but that's how you raise successful kids. Learn from your parenting mistakes and become better by it.

Discussion Questions

1. How do you plan to raise godly children?

2. How are you going to model Christ in the presence of your children?

Day 35

Dealing With In-laws

Scripture Meditation: "Honor your father and your mother, so that you may live long in the land the LORD your God is giving you" (*Exodus 20:12, NIV*).

In the previous section of the book, we discussed having boundaries within your marriage for you and your spouse. Boundaries are also necessary for others outside of your marriage, specifically your in-laws.

Everyone desires to have a great relationship with their in-laws; sometimes it happens, and sometimes it doesn't. Nonetheless, healthy boundaries are required so that the thoughts, ideas, and especially opinions of others do not affect your marriage in a negative way.

Even in-laws who have great intentions for you and your spouse can lure you into a tight space that is not healthy for your marriage.

We have already established that every marriage must be governed by the creator of marriage, which is God. As long as the two of you are governed by God and His principals, your marriage will work out fine. Yet there is no cookie-cutter solution for issues that arise in marriage. And there is no cookie-cutter way of a marriage flowing. Every couple is different because of the two very different individuals within the marriage. Your parents will have a number of influences and experiences that have shaped them and their perspective on the world.

Your in-laws are a vital part of your spouse's life. This makes them a crucial part of your life as well. Creating family harmony is possible—and it's very much worth the effort.

As a couple, you and your spouse are experiencing life together, and your experiences will shape the way you run your home, raise your children, and even the way you work through issues with your spouse. Boundaries are not an excuse to block out wise counsel from others. We all need wisdom and wise counsel from time to time. There is even a saying: "A wise man learns from the mistakes of others. A fool continuously makes mistakes to learn from them." We want you to be wise and learn from the mistakes of others, yet understand that even the mistakes of others must be filtered through how God has chosen to work and operate with you and your spouse.

If you have disagreements with your in-laws, your spouse may feel caught in the middle between parents and you. You, meanwhile, have obligations to in-laws and spouse — and children if you have any.

When you got married, you also became part of another family with its own set of expectations. You need to recognize and respect those — within limits.

If one spouse remains too dependent upon their parents, that needs to be addressed in a humble and straightforward way. If one spouse is blaming their in-laws for a disagreement the couple is experiencing, that should be dealt with too.

It can be very tempting to go to your comfort zone and tell your parents the problems that you are having with your spouse. Do not do this. The problem with telling close family members the issues you had with your spouse is, they will always remember the bad and the negative things that your spouse does. Your spouse may apologize to you, and then you issue forgiveness. But guess what? Your parents will still recall the negative, thoughtless actions of your spouse, whereas you have already forgiven them.

Let's set up a few fundamental boundaries that will help protect you:

#1 Do not run and discuss issues or problems immediately. Give yourselves time to work through the issues together. If it is not a life-and-death situation, then the two of you as committed persons within a lifetime covenant can be mature enough to discuss and resolve it.

#2 If you run into any issue or problem that seems unworkable, go to an unbiased person. That could be a pastor, a counselor/therapist, or even a mentor. You need someone who is willing to listen to both sides, and their main interest is the both of you, not one or the other.

#3 Do not accept everyone's opinion as fact. Opinions are just like armpits; everyone has them, and the ones that smell the worst are the ones that are the loudest. You and your spouse ought to discuss and weigh out both of your opinions and then find the middle ground. The two of you are very different, and coming together will take a level malleability that will constantly shape your future.

#4 Be ready to say "No." This can be tough, especially with loved ones who have supported you over the years, but if you don't establish the boundaries, you run the risk of losing your marriage. Rocky terms with in-laws never just go away. They fester and lend themselves to a rocky relationship with your spouse. It is better to have others upset with you for setting boundaries than have a rocky, unfulfilling marriage because of outsiders.

#5 Your marriage is your responsibility. You've committed yourself to your spouse and to God. God knows more than you and your spouse about your marriage. Pray and ask God for wisdom in your marriage. Ask God for wisdom with your spouse. Ask God for wisdom for you. What He will tell you will ALWAYS create a greater result than what you can come up with alone. Just in case you were wondering; yes, God cares and is concerned with your marriage. He will give you the strategies to not only make it work but make it fun and exciting.

Your in-laws are not your enemy. They could actually be parents you never had or add to the ones you do have. Cultivating a healthy relationship with your in-laws takes work and isn't an overnight affair.

Say happy birthday. Send a bouquet of flowers for their anniversary. Let them spend time with their grandkids. Don't mistreat them or talk bad about them in front of (or behind the back of) your spouse.

When you show contempt to your in-laws (even if your spouse does), it will always be taken personally.

Establish the relationship as much as you can without compromising your relationship. This decision will take you far in your marriage.

Discussion Questions

1. What can you do to cultivate the relationship with your in-laws?

2. Are there any boundaries that need to be set with the relationship with your in-laws that hasn't been set?

Day 36

Tips For Blended Families

Scripture Meditation: "But if anyone does not provide for his relatives, and especially for members of his household, he has denied the faith and is worse than an unbeliever" (*1 Timothy 5:18, ESV*).

Welcome to one of the most challenging yet rewarding aspects of your life. When families are joined together, it can be a great challenge due to a myriad of emotions, different personalities, varying levels of maturity that are connected together and must sync in order for this new family dynamic to work.

Unfortunately, as a counselor (Faith), I've seen too many people who go into the blended family situation underprepared. For blended families, love is not the only thing that is going to keep you together. You need a strategy and understanding of everyone involved. Blended families can be especially challenging for the children.

For the most part, most children want their biological parents to be together. When another person or parent is introduced, it can take a while for the child to adapt to and embrace the new person. That is why patience is key as well as emotional maturity from the parents. Often times, the parents will feel attacked or dismissed by the children of their spouse and take it personally. This is not the time to take anything personally. Most times, the problem the children have is not necessarily with the spouse but the dynamics of the relationship. This is a new person that they have to embrace, who is not their biological parent.

The Blender For The Blended Family

Our pastor, Dr. R. A. Vernon, gave a very beautiful illustration of how a blended family should function.

It takes 3–5 years for a family to blend.

Picture a blender with me. Let's say you want to make a smoothie. You add your kale, honey, milk, carrot, banana, and apple. Then you plug your blender into electric power. Cover the lid and hold it down. You press Start, and your smoothie gets mixed and is ready to nourish your body.

It's the same with a blended family — you are adding all sorts of items (strangers) with different personalities into the blender (home). You have to apply pressure (electricity) and cover the blender with a lid and hold it down (emotional and spiritual strength). It might take a smoothie 3 minutes to blend, but in real life, it might take your family 3–5 years to fully blend and function as one.

Parents, you must be able to separate your personal feelings from what is taking place and work toward the goal that you have to bring your families together. It would all be so simple if every blended family turned out as great as the Brady Bunch. Although that is TV, there is tremendous hope that can be derived from the show in regards to the joys of blended families.

There are some essentials to making blended families work:

#1. Have a strategy
Do not enter into a new marriage within a short span of time and expect the children to adapt immediately. It never works. Children have to have the 'option' of receiving that person. Give them time, introduce them to your potential spouse. Let them know that if they don't like the potential spouse, then you won't either. Let them know that they are not being *replaced*.

Let them know that they are as much involved in the relationship as you, the parent, are.

#2 Time is your friend

Time allows the children to get used to the person, love the person, have disagreements with the person, and see them as more than just a boyfriend or a temporary fix. With time, they can develop their own relationship with them, and when they are a good fit, marriage is inevitable, and the children will begin to say "Hey, when are we going to make this official?"

#3 After marriage, have family meetings

Sit down and discuss the goals of the house. Is one child graduating? Another child getting a job to purchase a car? One excelling in extracurricular activities? Or a parent transitioning to a new job? These are all factors that affect the family dynamics and should be openly discussed. Family meetings are similar to board meetings—as in everyone gets to hear each other's opinions and better understand each other's perspectives. From these meetings, relationships deepen and comradery builds.

Don't fall into the temptation of prioritizing your children before your new spouse.

Yes, your children are precious and important. Of course, they deserve your love, care, and attention. But make sure you are balancing your care of them with that of your marriage. By giving your spouse the attention they deserve, you are teaching your children to respect them (their new parent) also. By working hard at your marriage, you model success for them and prepare them for the future. That's a deeper, long-lasting kind of love. All children must be treated equally. Don't treat your children better than your stepchildren. Treat them all the same.

To keep your marriage strong, you must act as a united front in decisions related to the children. Both the parent and step-parent must not allow the children to play on their emotions or manipulate them. All decisions need to be made with both spouses acting as a team.

Blended families are a challenge, but it can work successfully.

Discussion Questions

1. Why is it difficult for blended families to blend?

2. In what ways can you strengthen your blended family?

SECRET TEN
Sex

Day 37

Developing Sexual Intimacy

Scripture Meditation: "So don't refuse sex to each other, unless you agree not to have sex for a little while, in order to spend time in prayer. Then Satan won't be able to tempt you because of your lack of self-control" (*1 Corinthians 7:5, CEV*).

Jones and Kierra's marriage was on the verge of folding up. Kierra felt unloved and insecure in her marriage. Her sexual desire for her husband had been declining steadily for months. Jones was getting frustrated by the day, wondering why Kierra didn't want to have sex with him.

"Why would I want to lay with someone who acts like I am secondary in their life?" she asked.

What he didn't realize is that sex is only meaningful to a woman when there is a mental or emotional stimulation or connection. He hadn't been showing her much attention and affection in the last eight months; hence the breakdown of sexual intimacy.

Intimacy is much more than physical; it's emotional and spiritual. When you accept your differences and complement each other, you'll discover the deepest intimacy you've ever known.

Sexual intimacy is necessary for a healthy relationship, yet sex is more meaningful to a woman if she feels loved and secured in the relationship.

A man needs sex. Women need sex too. Men often want sex more than women do. God made men like that. No medicine or drug can relieve and relax a man like good sex with the woman he loves.

Shaunti Feldhahn wrote in her bestselling book, *For Women Only*, "Sex plays a huge role in a man's self-confidence." A man can be having a horrible time at work, rejection in his industry and every other area can be going rotten—but if his wife wants him physically and affirms him in bed, he can handle the rest of the world with no problem. Conversely, if he gets the same impostor message at home, i.e., "You don't measure up. Don't touch me." It will devastate him far worse than any career blow.

Sex is one of the best ways a wife can affirm her husband and make him feel wanted and loved.

Most men started down the slippery slope toward sexual infidelity by flattery (another word for affirmation).

Many bosses have fallen into bed with their secretaries—and in such cases, the boss didn't even know when his heart began to warm up to her through the constant affirmations and flatteries.

Men love to be affirmed in what they do. Men enjoy when you praise their work. Just by telling your man "Honey, you're such a great Janitor. You add such great value to your company" means more to him that saying "I love you" five hundred times.

Men also love it when you affirm their provisions for the family. A man loathes it when his woman undervalues his contributions and provisions to the family supply chain. Even if you, the woman, are the major bread-winner in the house, learn to affirm your husband's ability to provide something to the family.

Affirming your husband helps to build sexual intimacy in his heart toward you. Conversely, loving and serving your spouse through their primary love language warms their heart toward you sexually.

Within marriage, servanthood is the only spirit that experiences true emotional, spiritual, or sexual intimacy. You simply can't be intimate with a selfish person. That means men and women both need to be sensitive to serving each other sexually. Our bodies belong to our spouse. This is not a license to abuse, but it is a license for use. We never withdraw our bodies from each other. We don't use our bodies as a weapon or a bargaining chip. We don't use sex to punish or manipulate.

Sexual fulfillment in marriage means saying to your spouse, "This is your body, and I will serve you with this body for the rest of our marriage." That is a very, very powerful thing.

God created sex. He loves to see His people enjoying the special gift He created. He wants us to be adventurous and enjoy sex in many different ways — not sinful ways, but in ways that give each other pleasure.

If you remove sex from your marriage, then you and your spouse are just overestimated roommates.

Sexual intimacy creates a bond that nothing else really can. Take the time to understand your spouse's sexual need and fulfill it.

Discussion Questions

1. How would you describe sexual intimacy in your marriage?

2. How can you please your spouse more sexually?

Day 38
Spice It Up

Scripture Meditation: "Marriage is honorable in every way, so husbands and wives should be faithful to each other. God will judge those who commit sexual sins, especially those who commit adultery" (*Hebrews 13:4, GW*).

One day, my wife came to me and said, "Babe, we need to spice up our sex life." She continued, "We need to make it more exciting and fun."

I knew she was telling the truth. We never wanted our sex life to be plain and uninteresting. So we decided to incorporate new sexual positions, sex games and trying different places in the house. We also decided to be more spontaneous with having sex instead of scheduling it. You see, when you have little children crying out for Mummy twenty-four hours a day, it can be tough to balance that with sexual intimacy.

God invented sex, and He never wanted your sex life to be sour and boring.

Sex is a gift you give to your spouse.

Everyone wants to go to a restaurant where the service was good and the food was hot and fresh.

You have a holy duty to God to fulfill the sexual need of your partner in marriage. Even when you are tired and feel like going to sleep, still find a way to fulfill their sexual need. We've told you over and over in this book that healthy marriages are ones where both partners are selfless and serving.

No Porn Allowed:

Never, ever allow porn or a third party into your sexual life. When you watch porn, you are fantasizing sex with someone else who is not your spouse. Even if you watch porn in the company of your spouse, you both are committing a sin before God by defiling your bed with another person. Sex in marriage is totally exclusive to two people. Porn watching can lead to porn addiction or worse. Many good marriages have been broken due to infidelities inspired form porn.

Try different things to spice your marriage. Try role-playing, surprises, and new sexual experimentation.

Because a man is moved by what he **sees**, his wife needs to both dress up for him and learn to flirt with him with her naked body. Men, by nature, love to see a woman naked. That is why men go to strip clubs. They don't go to strip clubs to have sex with women. No! They go to strip clubs to **see** women dance naked.

Imagine how much of a delight it is to your husband to see you naked around the house and bedroom?

By contrast, women are moved by what they **feel.** How you make her feel—by your muscles, biceps, or trips—is more important. She is not moved by your body; she is moved by how much you make her feel loved and secure.

For many women, sex is not what happens in the bedroom; it's how you treated her all day, your text messages, checking on her, helping her with the dishes, putting the kids to bed—these are the kinds of things that stimulate her sexually and make her ready for you.

Men derive pleasure from the physical outlook while women get enticed from passionate physical and emotional connection. As a woman, you need to learn what is pleasurable to your man. If he likes your legs, then wear short skirts or underwear around him.

Men love it when you initiate sex. Boost his ego. Tell him how good he is in bed. Tell him how much he pleases you. Give him a massage. Rub oil on him.

Discussion Questions

1. What are you going to start doing to spice up your marital sex life?

2. Discuss your sexual need with your spouse.

3. Do you feel sexually fulfilled in your marriage?

Day 39

Rekindle The Flame

Scripture Meditation: "She is beautiful and graceful, just like a deer; you should be attracted to her and stay deeply in love" (*Proverbs 5:19, CEV*).

Wow! We can't believe you have been reading this book from the first pages to this last section. Good job! We can tell that you are really serious about having a marriage from heaven.

Or did you skip the other pages just to get to the sex part? We hope not!

Let's state the obvious: Men want sex more than women in a relationship. Of course, we understand that in some marriages women are more sexual than their men. In God's perspective, the best and righteous way to enjoy sex is in the context of marriage.

There are many reasons why the rekindling of your sex life is necessary. Nothing is as dangerous to a marriage as a stale sex. Many couples have admitted that as they progressed in years in their marriage, it seemed like sexual chemistry and desires went flat. The excitement and urges they once felt was now only in their memories. Between responsibilities at home, demands from work or in business, kids, church roles, sports leagues, and having any type of social life, there is a lot that goes on that tries to hinder your sexual life.

Not to mention the unmentionables, which would be you and your spouse not looking exactly the same body-wise like when you first got married. When we speak to couples, often times the issue of body image comes up as a problem.

Women have the issue of their bodies changing remarkably to adhere to the new life of the baby that was growing within them.

While she was adapting to the baby growing, the father was adapting to the demands of having a pregnant wife using the comfort of food. These are normal issues that every couple in some form deals with.

The key is to deal with them and address them openly and honestly. Men, it will be very difficult for your wife to believe that you find her new body with its new markings sexy when you're constantly liking and admiring bodies on social media sites that look nothing like your wife's.

The same is applicable to the wives. Ladies, your husband will find it hard to believe that you still find him attractive when his once 6 pack has turned into a water cooler.

Your disseminating sentiments toward each of your bodies is affecting your ability to think sexually about one another. Sex was created by God to be enjoyed. When you are not enjoying it within the realm of which it was created, you forsake each other's needs. When either one of your needs isn't being met, there is an open door to outsiders infiltrating your marriage and meeting those needs.

Taking things back to the basics can help rekindle the flame between you and your spouse. If body image is a problem, you can do something about it — such as modifying your diet or simply implementing more physical activity into your routine.

Go on dates. If you're on a budget and with kids, pack a light dinner, sit in the car, turn on some tunes and enjoy each other.

Send each other thoughtful text messages throughout the day. Express your love and affection toward one another to illicit romantic feelings toward one another.

Get a hotel room for the weekend and hire a babysitter or family to watch the kids for a weekend vacation. No work allowed, and minimal technology is allowed.

Try a role reversal night. Sir, take care of your wife's nightly duties, and ladies, take over your husband's nightly duties. Women love to see men taking care of the children, and men don't mind their ladies showing a little muscle and taking out the trash.

The bottom line is to be intentional. If the thrill is gone, like the song says, you will need to get up and add logs to the fire, a little kerosene, and a match. The fire just won't light itself. You'll need to take steps to do it.

Sexual intimacy makes your spouse feel loved. It brings the both of you closer. There is a deep bond and connection with the wife—after having sex with her husband. Often times, men feel the most loved after being physically loved by their spouse, especially if their language is physical touch.

Therefore, it's unhealthy and ungodly for relationships when women use sex as a tool to get what they want or to punish their husbands. When that kind of behavior is happening, there is no real underlying connection to each other. There is no understanding of what that truly feels like for your spouse.

Continuous rejection of sexual intimacy makes your spouse feel unwanted and unloved. Sex is meant to be something that pulls you together, not as a manipulation tool or for control.

If you continually reject your spouse when it comes to sex, there will be major issues in your marriage. Rejecting being physically intimate with your spouse tells them that you do not desire them and do not want to be with them. On the other hand, when sex is made a priority, both you and your spouse will feel more loved. We dare you to try to make love to your spouse today!

Women, know that men love to be pursued and want to feel wanted sexually by their spouse.

Sexual intimacy is such a gift in marriage. It shouldn't be viewed as mere sex. When you and your spouse put sexual intimacy higher on the ladder in your marriage, you will both be happier and healthier. What is stopping you from doing that today? Maybe sit your spouse down and have an open conversation about your sex life today!

Discussion Questions

1. How would you describe sexual intimacy in your marriage?

2. Who enjoys sexual intimacy the most in your marriage?

3. How do you plan to spice up your sex life?

Day 40

Passionate Living

Scripture Meditation: "He who finds a wife finds a good thing, And obtains favor from the LORD" (*Proverbs 18:22, NKJV*).

Couples that win are the ones who passionately pursue one another. Romance is a part of any healthy relationship. Romance is indispensable in marriage.

Most couples who are not romantically compatible have relationship problems that lead to a breakup. Passion and chemistry are very important in building a successful relationship. There has to be a romantic attraction between the both of you. In fact, the stronger the romantic compatibility between you both, the better. *Romantic and emotional needs are the major reasons women cheat in a relationship. Women do not often cheat because of sexual needs; they cheat because of the lack of emotional and romantic needs in their relationship.*

When he stops listening to her, bringing her flowers, taking her out on date nights, engaging her emotionally, he leaves her open and vulnerable to romantic affairs.

Intimacy means closeness on the inside, not just on the outside. If you're going to have true closeness in your marriage, you have to be able to know each other and have unhindered access without fear.

I think of intimacy in terms of the acronym INVEST: Intimacy Necessitates Value, Energy, Sacrifice, and Trust.

Here are some clues that you are feeling romantic compatibility with your spouse:

1. You always want to talk to them and be in their presence.
2. You miss them when they are unavailable.
3. The loved person takes on a 'special meaning' in your life.
4. Intrusive, romantic and sexual thinking and feelings about the loved person.
5. You begin to make excuses and overlook his/her negative traits.

6. A longing for emotional reciprocity coupled with the desire to achieve emotional union with the loved person.
7. Emotional dependency on the relationship with the loved person.
8. A powerful sense of empathy toward the loved person ... and a willingness to sacrifice for them.
9. A reordering of daily priorities to be with the loved one ... including changing one's clothing, mannerisms, habits, or daily structure.
10. Intensification of passionate feelings about the loved one.

REGISTER FOR 40 DAYS MARRIAGE BOOK CAMP

What about if you had the nation's leading marriage and relationship coaches to be your personal marriage mentors for 40 days? What is the value of that? PRICELESS.

Ultimate Marriage & Relationship Coaching for
40 Consecutive days:
- Daily video coaching
- Personalized email
- Bible verse for the day
- Discussion questions & Much More to help you have HEAVEN in your marriage.

www.MarriageFromHeaven.tv